Illustrated Men

0.1 Lamont O'Neal—Fashion illustration—Gucci.

Illustrated Men

Drawing and Rendering the Male Fashion Figure

Lamont O'Neal

BLOOMSBURY VISUAL ARTS
LONDON · NEW YORK · OXFORD · NEW DELHI · SYDNEY

BLOOMSBURY VISUAL ARTS
Bloomsbury Publishing Plc
50 Bedford Square, London, WC1B 3DP, UK
1385 Broadway, New York, NY 10018, USA
29 Earlsfort Terrace, Dublin 2, Ireland

BLOOMSBURY, BLOOMSBURY VISUAL ARTS and the Diana logo are
trademarks of Bloomsbury Publishing Plc

First published in Great Britain 2023

Cover design by Steven Lau
Cover illustration by Lamont O'Neal

A catalogue record for this book is available from the British Library.

Library of Congress Cataloging-in-Publication Data
Names: O'Neal, Lamont, author.
Title: Illustrated men : drawing and rendering the male fashion figure / Lamont O'Neal.
Description: London : Bloomsbury Visual Arts, 2023. | Summary: "The ultimate guide to
drawing and rendering the male fashion figure"– Provided by publisher.
Identifiers: LCCN 2022012053 (print) | LCCN 2022012054 (ebook) |
ISBN 9781350125469 (paperback) | ISBN 9781350125476 (hardback) |
ISBN 9781350125490 (ebook) | ISBN 9781350125483 (pdf)
Subjects: LCSH: Fashion drawing–Technique. | Men in art.
Classification: LCC TT509 .O54 2023 (print) | LCC TT509 (ebook) |
DDC 741.6/72–dc23/eng/20220819
LC record available at https://lccn.loc.gov/2022012053
LC ebook record available at https://lccn.loc.gov/2022012054

ISBN: HB: 978-1-3501-2547-6
          PB: 978-1-3501-2546-9
          ePDF: 978-1-3501-2548-3
          eBook: 978-1-3501-2549-0

Typeset by Integra Software Services Pvt. Ltd.
Printed and bound in India.

To find out more about our authors and books visit www.bloomsbury.com
and sign up for our newsletters.

For Tim

CONTENTS

Costume trompe l'œil
veste/gilet en flanelle
gris

Pantalon baggy en
flanelle gris

Chemise en cotton blanc
avec nœud.

Pantalon
baggy
en flanelle
gris

inspiration
"sniper"

ACKNOWLEDGMENTS

I am very grateful to the many people who have made this book possible. Thanks to my publisher Georgia Kennedy, my editors Faith Marsland and Belinda Campbell, and others at Bloomsbury for their unwavering support and encouragement. For a first-time author, one couldn't ask for a better team.

I was also lucky enough to have access to an entire art department in my long-time friend, Steven Lau. Steven approached this project with his customary intelligence, zeal, and diligence, combining his role of creative director with that of copy editor, illustrator, researcher, and art director. I can't imagine this book without his input.

I'd also like to thank Mary Capozzi, my not-so-secret managing editor. She was responsible for bringing this book to completion.

Thanks to Karen Trivette and April Calahan at the Fashion Institute of Technology's Special Collections, Gladys Marcus Library and Goodman Resource Center, for their expert help and generous assistance.

Grateful thanks to Shireen Soliman and Deb Kasten for their constructive input and insight. They helped to make this a better book than it might have been.

Thanks to Steven Stipelman, who suggested this project, for his support and guidance. It is because of him that this book exists.

Thank you to all the artists and designers who so generously contributed their work. My aim was to show the variety and breadth of menswear art and that would not have been possible without their kind and enthusiastic participation. To Renaldo Barnette and George Gozum, a special thanks for their steadfast support.

A posthumous thank you to Eric Bentley, mentor and friend, for helping me to become a writer. He envisioned this book decades before it happened.

And never last, nor least: thanks to my husband, Tim Stauffer, whose steady support, good humor, and infinite patience allowed me to complete this book.

Figure 0.1 Francisco J. Cortes.

PREFACE

I've been drawing all my life. My earliest memory of making art was an uncommissioned crayon mural on my mother's kitchen wall. The review was emphatically negative. But despite that unpromising beginning, I later went to an art high school, and then to an art college. Over the years, as a commercial artist and designer, I've created fashion illustrations for department stores, magazines, book publishers, fashion designers, and advertising agencies. I also teach.

Teaching, like drawing, is a form of communication, and in many ways this book is an extension of my classes. Most people are terrified of drawing, and my aim, as an instructor, has always been to demystify the process of drawing: to show that if I can do it, then the student could do it, too. As a faculty member at the Fashion Institute of Technology and having taught at Parsons School of Design and Moore College of Art, my approach to menswear illustration, not surprisingly, is a distillation of my experiences as an artist and a teacher. My goal as an instructor has always been to help the student better express themselves. This means refining and polishing whatever skill or creativity the burgeoning illustrator or designer already has.

That menswear fashion illustration has received less attention than women's fashion illustration is not too surprising. Until fifty years ago, men's fashion was considered not only less interesting, but also slightly irrelevant. Fashion has always been considered feminine, frivolous, and vaguely artistic, traits that were the opposite of the masculine ideal. If there were no such thing as men's fashion, then men's fashion illustration couldn't exist. Thankfully, however, men's fashion and men's fashion art does exist, and always has in some form—and certainly now more than ever. The proof is in the spending. Worldwide revenue from menswear reached an estimated $154 billion from 2020 to 2024. Menswear is big business, so it follows that designing menswear and illustrating menswear are important aspects of the business. And both have everything to do with drawing.

Everyone at some point in their childhood has drawn something. This appears to happen in all cultures at roughly the same time in a child's development and seems to be an important part of human maturation. At an early stage, when we're drawing, we are seeing and holding images, and transforming the images into symbols. If you asked a five-year-old to draw their house, they would draw a square with a triangle on top and a vertical rectangle as a chimney, even if they lived in an apartment. The child is drawing what they *know*, as opposed to what they see. Their visual vocabulary is too limited for anything too specific, hence the symbols. Many beginning art students have trouble going beyond this stage. They cannot draw representationally: They need guidance. Drawing isn't something that can be learned quickly, and being self-taught has its own limitations. That is why there are schools, classes, and, yes, books. We learn to draw by drawing, but also by instruction.

The primary goal of this book is the drawing and rendering of the male fashion figure, so drawing fundamentals such as anatomy and proportion are stressed during the first third of the book. Later chapters will focus on working methods, garment drawing, poses, and how they relate to a garment, and the various media—markers, watercolor, color pencil, etc.—used in rendering the clothed figure. Topics such as individual style and the changing views of men's fashion are examined. Digital rendering of the figure is also discussed. The intention of the book is to be both a textbook and a reference source. In short, *Illustrated Men* will be, I hope, the equivalent of a year in a men's fashion art class. It is also my hope that this book will help any artist or designer to create the type of menswear art that truly reflects their aims and wishes.

A Final Note: Please be aware that I have used American terminology throughout the book. For example, sneakers instead of trainers; sweaters instead of jumpers; suspenders instead of braces; turtlenecks instead of polo necks; and vests instead of waistcoats.

Introduction

The Fashionable Male: A Brief History in Four Figures

Style and fashion are not the same thing. If fashion is what is currently regarded as "in style," then personal style is the way in which one wears one's clothes. It is the way in which we express our individuality. Clothes are rarely just garments, but often signifiers of our identity or, more precisely, how we wish to be perceived. This is reflected in the adage "Clothes make the man." All through history a man's clothes have reflected his class, nationality, taste, and politics. We can see a society's idea of what a man should be, and how men did or did not conform to this idea, reflected in past and contemporary images. Nowhere is this more obvious than in the changing look of menswear. In this chapter I will briefly explore the sartorial evolution of menswear through several men of fashion, from the 18th century's Beau Brummell to the late 20th-century Sean "Puffy" Combs.

Figure I.1 Portrait of George 'Beau' Brummell (1778-1849) by Robert Dighton. Bridgeman Images.

BEAU BRUMMELL (1778–1840)

Throughout history, men were supposed to wear clothes that underscored the current society's idea of masculinity, and for the most part that meant being seen as strong, resolute, and in control. In a word, manly. So, it is no wonder that military garb was such a potent source of inspiration for menswear throughout Western history. Particularly for those in power, clothes were meant to convey unquestioned authority, and since most societies were hierarchical—the king and queen, then dukes, then lords, etc.—good taste was upper class, and bad taste was lower class. Men's clothing was often dictated according to one's social rank and privilege.

In late 18th-century France and England, it was only with the rise of the middle class that the social ambitions of the upwardly mobile changed: Men no longer dressed according to their social rank, as custom had long dictated, but rather according to the rank they aspired to. In this era, men's fashion became more practical and less extravagant. This move to more restrained and sober clothing reflected not only the spirit of the democratic aims of the French and American Revolutions, but also the values, and the growing power, of the new, industrious, and religious bourgeoisie. And yet, there were contradictions. If male dress was often dark and austere—black was the dominant color for men's clothing in the 19th century—there were still men who wanted to shine in a big way, and so the Dandy was born.

Dandies were non-conformists who rejected bourgeois values. They were devoted solely to their own aesthetic independence. As Thomas Carlyle wrote, "A Dandy is a clothes-wearing Man, a Man whose trade, office and existence consists in the wearing of clothes." Fashion, and how one appeared, was their only interest. They had the seemingly carefree and lazy lifestyle of the poor Bohemians, but with inherited money. They weren't aristocrats, even as they emulated them; Dandies affected a conspicuous frivolity. At best, they made a religion out of aesthetics; at worst, they squandered fortunes doing nothing in particular. But they did it with style; and London, where European men interested in fashion took their cues, was their capital.

If English fashion influenced all of Europe, then Beau Brummell was Europe's first male trendsetter, and its first Dandy of consequence. George Bryan Brummell (1778–1840) was a commoner who personified a type of male elegance that was unmistakably different from the aristocrats'. Living on a sizable inheritance, he was said to have had three hairdressers, several glove makers, and the most expensive and exclusive tailors in London. He refused to wear jewelry or perfume and was obsessed with cleanliness. The pristine way he wore his starched white linen shirts and cravats was the stuff of legend. However, it was Brummell's friendship with, and his role as adviser to the court of, the Prince of

Wales (the Prince Regent and later King George IV) that helped to widely spread his influence in England and France.

The few existing portraits of Brummell don't depict him as being overly attractive—Brummell's nickname, Beau, was for his style of dress, not his physical beauty—yet his appeal was magnetic. His usual daytime outfit consisted of a dark blue frock coat, a fawn-colored chamois vest, light-colored trousers or breeches of suede, and soft Hessian boots—polished, allegedly, with champagne! In the evening he wore a blue suit with matching buttons, white vest, tight pants buttoned at the instep, and silk stockings with matching pumps. To our modern eyes his clothes seem anything but dramatic, but Brummell's dress was a radical break from the then popular continental style of French and Italian men. They wore powdered wigs, make-up, buckled shoes, perfume, and elaborately embroidered colored silks and satins—all part of most European court fashions. By comparison, Brummell's relatively austere and simple dress was revolutionary. His contribution to modern male dressing was in taking the practical clothing of a military officer—coat, waistcoat, and breeches—and simplifying it for civilian use.

By 1816, Brummell was a changed man. He had fallen from grace with the Prince Regent after a rude remark and, because of gambling, was heavily in debt. He fled his creditors and the prince by escaping to France. There he lived the remainder of his life in grueling poverty, a steep fall from the exalted existence he had lived earlier, finally dying in an asylum in 1840.

Beau Brummell is credited with establishing a dress code that had nothing to do with class or social rank. His simpler style of a fitted plain dark coat, pristine white shirt, and cravat soon became the basis for the modern-day suit and tie. He gave men across all social classes a type of male elegance distinct from the courtly restrictions of the aristocracy. His dress code would soon evolve into a more egalitarian expression of what constituted a fashionable male. And his style of sartorial restraint and disciplined modesty became an archetype of the modern gentleman.

EDWARD VIII, FORMER KING OF ENGLAND

But what does "modern" mean? For many in the 1920s, the modern world was born at the end of the First World War. To be modern, then, was to reject anything of the Victorian Era, and this naturally included clothing. While the mature, British, pre-First World War generation returned to their stiff and conservative Savile Row suits, the younger, post-war generation wanted something different, something that reflected the ease and comfort they associated with modernity. The young students back then preferred the Oxford and Cambridge style of baggy flannels (28-inch bottoms!), Fair Isle sweater vests, and soft-collared shirts. They rejected the Victorian principle of rigidly dressing for a specific time of day; but they were hardly anarchists. They were still very much a part of the English gentry, so their character was shaped by their membership in a class whose members all spoke the same slang and went to the same universities, clubs, and tailors. While this was a world of strict hierarchy, with detailed codes of behavior, there was still some room for self-expression, and this pushing of boundaries, along with an innate conservatism, was just the sort of environment that bred rebellion. It was out of this background, and his reaction to it, that the Prince of Wales emerged as a fashion icon of the 1920s and beyond.

Edward Albert Christian George Andrew Patrick David (1894–1972) was the great grandson of Queen Victoria, and heir to the British throne. At one time he was known as the Prince of Wales; following the death of his father, George V, in 1936, he became Edward VIII. He later abdicated the throne to marry Wallis Simpson, an American divorcée; the ex-king then became the Duke of Windsor. The complex and controversial life of the duke is beyond the scope of this brief history—we are only interested in his contribution to male fashion, and in that there is little to dispute.

From a young age, the prince was reared in a buttoned-up childhood. His father was a conservative monarch who belonged, unapologetically, to the late 19th century; the old king believed in detailed codes of behavior, and an adherence to a strict hierarchy. Not surprisingly,

Figure I.2 The Duke of Windsor © SZ Photo / Scherl / Bridgeman Images.

the young prince rebelled against these social restrictions. His acts of rebellion included going against custom when it came to dress; like many of his age group, he hated what he perceived as the rigid formal dress of his father's generation. He loathed ceremonial dress.

In his private life the prince began to dress for comfort and ease, wearing roomy jackets with unpadded shoulders and pockets, wide pants, soft collars, sweater vests, and belts instead of suspenders. He was one of the first men in the 1930s to wear an unlined, unconstructed jacket; in public he wore berets and scarves. His signature silhouette was the drape cut, a softly constructed jacket paired with a voluminous chest area, a natural shoulder, and a high-cut, waisted, pleated trouser. Unafraid of censure, he wore unconventional patterns, loud checked tweeds, plaids, checks, and stripes—vivid examples of his taste. If the mixing of unusual colors or patterns occasionally made some people shudder, well, royalty has its privileges. In 1933, the prince wore a double-breasted jacket in a houndstooth fabric, then a material usually found in casual single-breasted jackets. He abandoned jewelry, vests, and hats (other than the aforementioned beret and an occasional bowler). He favored unstarched shirt cuffs for evening wear, and tab collars for formal wear. He also insisted on not wearing gloves while dancing. These sartorial choices were examples of an escape from royal restraint. While the prince was by no means a radical—in fact, given his position, one could hardly expect him to be anything other than conservative—he was able to add a personal, even eccentric touch to his wardrobe that, when coupled with the aura of privilege, tradition, and innovation, gave his appearance a lively, idiosyncratic undertone that the public viewed as modern. As a result, the prince seemed a more accessible royal, and his official wardrobe

Figure I.3 The Duke of Windsor, Bridgeman Images.

was viewed as the first word in male fashion. But it wasn't until he made his trip to the United States, in 1924, that he became a media star and fashion icon.

After the First World War, the United States became a world power and industrial leader and, with its sizable and relatively affluent population, the most influential nation. However, despite America's clout, British supremacy in menswear remained unchallenged: Savile Row's bespoke suits still represented the pinnacle of male style. During his visit, the Prince of Wales was viewed as not only an ambassador of British fashion, but also an example of the new modern man. He became the first male celebrity to sell clothes, as in "worn by the Prince of Wales." One did not need to be an Anglophile to be impressed. Young Americans could relate to his easy-going style and his image of comfort and ease. For many, the Duke of Windsor became an archetype of the modern gentleman. No wonder, then, that the prince's particular brand of casual stylishness became a major influence on American men in the 1930s, and for several decades afterwards. His unique brand of male elegance, made more attractive by coming from British tradition, was soon reflected in the look of any man with a claim to fashion. Hollywood icons such as Cary Grant and Fred Astaire, and even artists such as W. Somerset Maugham and Jean Cocteau, were all influenced by the Prince of Wales cult. We can still see the British upper-class look today, in the imagery and clothes of long-established companies such as Brooks Brothers, J. Press, Turnbull & Asser, Aquascutum, and Ralph Lauren, and on the students at certain American universities. Although the Duke of Windsor might well have blanched at being described as "preppy," his once radical style of dress has become "classic," the sort of look we expect from captains of industry, politicians, and certain conservative men of style.

THE BEATLES

When we think of iconic men of style, we tend to think of individuals: people who, through dint of charisma and taste, change the way we think about clothes and how to wear them. It is rare that a group can project any message other than uniformity. But there are exceptions, and within the context of menswear in the 1960s,

no group had a stronger effect on male fashion than the Beatles. They were not fashion designers or models. Nor were they movie stars, at least not primarily, but their impact on men's fashion was seismic. For men of a certain age, they were unimpeachable role models. They not only revolutionized popular music; they helped to expand the ways in which a man could choose to appear. As their images as counter-culture deities evolved over the decade, they began to not only influence but also mirror the shifting nature of men's fashion, politics, and presentation that was occurring in their young audiences.

The most popular and influential rock band of the 20th century was formed in 1960; the members were John Lennon (1940–80), Paul McCartney (1942–), George Harrison (1943–2001), and Ringo Starr (1940–). All the Beatles were born in Liverpool, an industrial shipping port in North England, and all came from working-class families. McCartney met John Lennon (and Stuart Sutcliffe), then known as the Quarrymen, in 1957, at the age of fifteen. George Harrison joined a year later, and Ringo was added after they dismissed their original drummer. In the beginning they were what we would describe, today, as a garage band: a group of teenagers who, in their spare time and away from school, got together to make music. Their early look consisted of greasy pompadours, leather jackets, stovepipe jeans, and boots. The style was suggestive of motorcycles, rock 'n' roll, and rough bad boys. This was not only an homage to their heroes, Elvis Presley and Gene Vincent, but also a sartorial declaration of their teenage non-conformity. This would change once Brian Epstein (1934–67) became their manager.

It was Epstein who suggested that they might be more successful if they looked more professional, which in England, at the time, meant well

Figure I.4 The Beatles, Bridgeman Images.

groomed. The Beatles' iconic presentation in 1962 of matching collarless suits, Chelsea boots, and mop-top hair became a "look" that managed to convey both polish and a certain rebelliousness. The gray suits—piped in black and worn with thin black ties—were designed by London tailor Dougie Millings and inspired by Pierre Cardin's 1960 menswear designs; Cardin was one of the first designers of menswear to emerge during the late 1950s and early 1960s. This minimalist look would epitomize the "Mod" style of early British fashion—Mod being short for Modern—and was a response to wider trends in fashion, art, and graphic design. Mod fashion represented the aspirations of young working-class men and women who patterned themselves after modern jazz (Miles Davis, Dave Brubeck, Modern Jazz Quartet, etc.), beatniks, and the Left Bank intellectuals in Paris, French-style Mods known as *minets*, or "trendies." For young men growing up in Britain after the Second World War, the need to escape the post-war grayness and depravations of the country motivated many to look abroad to French and American popular culture for inspiration. Viewed in that context, the Beatles' clothes from 1962 to 1964 were both a nod to British tailoring and a touch of the Gallic avant-garde.

After their initial phenomenal success, the Beatles entered a period of what might be termed introspection. They were superstars, and that success inevitably brought more self-confidence and a greater need for autonomy. If the earlier clothes were a nod to group cohesion and a recognition of the need to conform to established showbiz norms, their clothes now reflected maturity and individuality. This period from 1964 to 1966, best exemplified by the *Rubber Soul* album cover, saw them wearing brown suede jackets, turtlenecks, and brighter colors and patterns. They wore casual jeans, but now these were paired with sports jackets and T-shirts. One might describe the look as "preppy beatnik": a collegiate look, but with an edge. The group look was slowly developing into a collection of subtle individual styles. In fact, it was a look that could be described as transitional.

For most of the 20th century, men's fashion had moved at a glacial pace. Men bought suits off-the-rack, or, if they had the means, acquired a bespoke suit from a tailor. Until the late 1950s, menswear designers simply didn't exist. Changes in men's design from the late 1920s to the 1950s were more about the shoulder-width of a jacket, or the drape of a pant, than a revolutionary new look; for example, the 1940s' only major contribution to menswear was synthetic fabrics. But 1966 proved to be an exception. By the mid-1960s, London in general, and Carnaby Street in particular, seemed to pulse with youthful energy and excitement. There was a new attitude in male dress, one in which bold color, improvisation, and androgyny reigned. Menswear influencers like retailer John Stephen and Michael Fish, a designer for Turnbull & Asser, began to reference 18th-century dandyism and experiment with brightly colored suits, paisley ties, and scarves. Consciousness-expanding drugs such as LSD, popularized by Timothy Leary, played a part in the look of this current image. The so-called "Peacock Revolution" can be seen in the acid-soaked imagery of the Beatles' album cover for *Sgt. Pepper's Lonely Hearts Club Band* (1967), and in their animated film, *Yellow Submarine*. Gone were the dull, dark, conventional clothes of the older generation; now the idea was to play with unconventional ideas of class and gender roles, to explore color and texture. On the cover of *Sgt. Pepper's*, the Beatles are dressed in vintage regimental uniforms, but the colors are bright and saturated. Ringo's jacket is pink satin, John's is lime green, Paul's is sky blue, and George's is scarlet. Their epaulets and frogs (frogs, or frog-gings, are decorative cords or braids with intricate knots and loops) are bright gold and silver, and their military braids are pink, sunflower yellow, and baby blue. John has a daisy on his right shoulder, along with various colorful medals. Everyone's hair is longer and shaggier, and all are wearing mustaches. The background photograph is a startling neon canary yellow. Here, and in photos of the group outside of the studio, the usual clichés of masculinity were abandoned in favor of adopting stereotypical "feminine" colors for their wardrobe and sporting long hair. There was a defiant casualness with which this androg-yny was maintained: snug-fitting, low-waist trousers (also known as hip huggers) were worn, along with brightly colored shirts in pink, yellow, and lilac. Fitted Edwardian and Nehru jack-ets in plush velvets, vibrant satins, and brocades were all the rage, and suddenly, jewelry for men became fashionable: rings, medallions, beads, and bangles. Lennon, who earlier refused to wear glasses when he was photographed, now wore them unashamedly. The Beatles were now camp and psychedelic icons. This new and extravagant sartorial freedom suggested a youthful hedonism that would slowly and stealthily be transformed into the last fashion stage of the late 1960s: the hippie.

The hippie, with his long hair, flowered shirt, and bell-bottomed jeans, remains as much a cultural stereotype as the gin-guzzling flappers of the 1920s. The look, which began in the United States in Haight-Ashbury, San Francisco, came out of the social movements of the time—the civil rights and anti-Vietnam War movements—and the beatnik tradition of non-conformism. Silk scarves, shaggy Afghan coats, sandals, and a

multitude of beads became symbols of a new counter-culture: Natural fabrics were preferable to synthetics, flea markets were preferred over department stores. Soon the popularity of frayed and patched jeans became an implicit criticism of mid-century American consumerism and a personal expression of individuality. All of this is visible on the album covers of the *White Album*, *Abbey Road*, and *Let It Be*, and in the numerous photos of the Beatles from 1968 to 1970. Clad in T-shirts, bell-bottoms, vests, silk shirts, hats, and fur coats, their clothes during this period reflected both the current state of popular culture and what had happened to the band. After ten years, the Beatles were no longer a coordinated band, but a group of unique individuals, each dressing to please himself.

The Beatles disbanded in 1969 (though this was not officially announced until 1970). Although the four members all had varying degrees of solo success, it is as a group that they exist as unique and dynamic images of the 1960s. Like all potent cultural icons, they represented an idealized image of who we thought we were, or what we thought we could be.

The 1970s saw the birth of the celebrity menswear designer. Pierre Cardin might have been the first, in 1959, but he was soon followed in the UK by menswear designers like Hardy Amies and Tommy Nutter. Amies represented the establishment with his reliably elegant Savile Row suits, while Nutter made his impact with celebrity rock stars like Mick Jagger and David Bowie. While both designers were wildly influ-ential, their commercial impact was limited: Neither was able to extend his commercial reach beyond the UK (though Tommy Nutter contin-ued his menswear influence by later mentoring Ozwald Boateng). It would not be until the next decade that menswear powerhouses like Giorgio

Figure I.6 Sean "Diddy" Combs attends the 2022 Billboard Music Awards. Photo by Mindy Small/FilmMagic courtesy of Getty Images.

Armani, Hugo Boss, and Ralph Lauren would dominate the male fashion world.

SEAN JOHN COMBS, AKA PUFF DADDY

By the 1980s, performers, musicians, singers, and actors were the ultimate fashion role models, and through the power and reach of modern media—their movies, television, records, and radio—they had a potential audience of tens of millions. With this new ability to command almost universal attention, performers became more adept at creating outsized public personas

Figure I.5 Men's fashion through the ages (1910-2010).

that not only dazzled but also provoked: Think of David Bowie, Elton John, Prince, or Michael Jackson. Such savvy entertainers developed an acute awareness of the power of clothing. They grasped the idea that clothes could convey more than just glamour or fantasy, but also shifting ideas of sexuality, ethnicity, class, and politics. For artists whose work was meant to provoke and challenge, clothes helped to illustrate a particular point of view. Nowhere was this more obvious than in the rap and hip-hop artists of the late 20th century.

Hip-hop began as the music of the marginalized. It was born in the American urban ghettos of poor and working-class black youth who grew up amid hardship and crime. Like the 1970s punk scene in the UK, it was protest music by the angry and disillusioned. Early rap performers wore the same streetwear that their audiences wore: tracksuits, baggy jeans, hooded sweatshirts, Timberland boots, and baseball caps—sportswear that was durable and affordable. As hip-hop artists became more successful, they began to wear the same clothing, but with luxury brand logos that signaled status. This had the effect of calling attention to their new-found wealth, while also raising a middle finger to an ambivalent, if not hostile, white establishment. However, whatever love early rappers might have had for these brands, it was rarely, if ever, reciprocated. Soon, many black artists were made to feel unwelcome in certain high-end designer stores. Not surprisingly, this created a certain tension. The more inaccessible the luxury brands, the more desirable they became. Eventually, entrepreneurial tailors like Dapper Dan (Daniel R. Day) began to illegally use these same logos, printing them on fabrics that would then be made into one-of-a-kind pieces for black celebrities and performers. Dan's dazzling creations combined name-brand cachet with streetwise black pride. These clothes not only symbolized black creativity and black style; they also became compelling statements of economic power and self-realization. Of course, once rap music became popular to wider white audiences, it was inevitable that the clothing style of black hip-hop artists would be co-opted and mass-produced. By the mid-1990s Tommy Hilfiger, Ralph Lauren, and others began to market the same baggy jeans and leather jackets that many viewed as suspect just a few years before. Response to this marketing gave rise to Sean "Puffy" Combs and the emergence of a hip-hop aesthetic in menswear.

Sean John Combs (1969–), also known as Puff Daddy, P. Diddy, Puffy, or Diddy—all variations on a childhood nickname—was born in New York City but raised in Mount Vernon, New York. He attended Howard University, majoring in business, with the intention of becoming both a performer and an entrepreneur. He later dropped out of Howard to become Uptown Record's chief talent scout. In 1993 Combs left Uptown Records and started Bad Boy Entertainment. The ensuing years showcased him as a spectacularly successful rapper, singer, songwriter, record producer, actor, and, last but not least, menswear designer. In 1998 he created Sean John, his menswear clothing line. Inspired by Tommy Hilfiger and Ralph Lauren (going so far as to hire executive Jeffrey Tweedy away from Lauren), along with his love of streetwear, he created a menswear line that helped to integrate hip-hop style into the broader fashion world. Sean John was certainly not the first clothing line to reflect a hip-hop or black sensibility, but it was the first to combine an extravagant hip-hop aesthetic with a mass-market approach. Combs didn't go to design school, but he was certainly a student of fashion, and like many

Figure I.7 Sean "Diddy" Combs. Photo by Ethan Miller/Getty Images.

designers, his clothes reflected both who he was, and who he aspired to be. His eponymous line was a mash-up of urban swagger and Las Vegas panache, but with activist undertones. Coming down the runway of Combs's first show were luxurious fur coats worn over oversized sleeveless T-shirts and track pants, bucket hats worn with gold medallions and leather pants, baseball caps and cashmere hoodies over cropped pants and sneakers, and all worn by young black and brown models. This imaginative combination of high and low reflected both the casualization of modern menswear and the multiculturalism of the new millennials.

Through Combs, and others like Phat Farm, FUBU, and Roc-a-Wear, hip-hop fashion was responsible for the elevation of streetwear.

Combs contributed to a way of dressing that is recognizable as early 21st-century menswear just as top hats and tuxedos represented the ideal man of the 1920s. Combs was first nominated for a Council of Fashion Designers of America (CFDA) award in 2000, finally winning the award in 2004. Today, he has eschewed the lavish fabrics and furs of the early 2000s for mass-produced clothing for a younger generation. His more affordable line consists of sportswear staples for the average young man: polo shirts, jeans, baseball caps, watches, footwear, fragrance, and suits. Like many designers before him, he co-opted a counter-culture aesthetic, dressed it up, mass-produced it, and resold it to the masses: all with a heavy dose of race pride. Combs's achievements made the space available to black designers, from Kanye West and Pharrell Williams to Virgil Abloh and Olivier Rousteing. As if further proof of his success was needed, in 2018 Sean John Combs was reported to be the second richest hip-hop artist in America, with an estimated wealth of US $825 million.

From Beau Brummell's influential modernization of 18th-century dress to Sean Combs's celebration and mass-marketing of the hip-hop or urban aesthetic, each of the men discussed here has contributed to the way men dress today. We have seen how the evolving definition of masculinity and the societal influences of class, politics, gender, and ethnicity are made manifest in the clothing of men throughout history. A host of men, not limited to Western Europe or those examined here, have challenged, reinvented, and reinterpreted menswear and, by extension, contributed to what a fashionable modern man looks like today.

1

Men's Fashion Illustration: An Overview

ashion illustration as a profession was born out of necessity. While cameras and the photographic process had improved during the 19th century, by 1900 it was still difficult to photograph subjects in color, and even more problematic to print and reproduce them; replicating the black lines and flat colors of fashion drawings was less complicated (full color reproduction would not be possible until the early 1930s). Without the demands of advertising, and the limitations of photography, fashion illustration might never have flourished.

Artists have been drawing and painting beautiful people in beautiful clothes since the beginning of time, but fashion illustration as a distinct career in general, and men's fashion illustration in particular, is a comparatively new phenomenon. The earliest forms of fashion illustration were utilitarian. These simple

Figure 1.1 *GQ*, 1984/Antonio. The Estate & Archives of Antonio Lopez and Juan Ramos.

drawings were usually for tailors or dressmakers to help explain the turn of a collar or the fitting of a sleeve; the idea of using these technical aids to express a mood or a style would never have occurred to anyone. Nevertheless, images of fashionable men are hardly new.

Though historians trace the general public's interest in men's fashion at least as far back as the 16th century, earlier depictions of men's fashions can be found in the paintings, sculptures, and manuscripts of military heroes and assorted nobility. The great and the good—and the not so good—have always wanted to be remembered for posterity, and since not everyone can build a pyramid, a portrait has often been used as a sensible alternative. Often, these idealized images seemed more focused on clothes and accessories as markers of rank and privilege than an exact likeness of the sitter. A typical portrait, or bust, was intended to invoke veneration or awe; fashion trends seemed beside the point. Joshua

Figure 1.2 Richard Peers Symons by Joshua Reynolds, 1770–1. © Cincinnati Art Museum / Museum Purchase / Bridgeman Images.

Reynolds's portrait of Richard Peers Symons, MP (later a baronet) is a perfect example.

Mr. Symons was twenty-five at the time of this painting, yet he looks older, not in age, but in manner. There is, in his pose, natural nobility. He is dressed in a dove-gray suit of satin trimmed in silver brocade, and while he is undoubtedly fashionable, he is not a Dandy. The classical background, the Farnese Hercules and the Roman Temple, the adoring hound—all suggest a cultured and sophisticated world traveler comfortable with his exalted place in the world. To be sure, this has more to do with the talent

and discreet flattery of Reynolds than anything resembling reality. But it is a delightful portrait of an aristocrat and, one could argue, a kind of fashion illustration. Which begs the question: Who needs fashion when you are above it? For much of human history, images of royalty and the aristocracy suggested they were both in and beyond fashion. It is only with the invention of the printing press that this assumption began to change.

Johannes Gutenberg's movable printing press in 1454 was the technological shift that made the first printed fashion illustrations possible. Because of this invention, and the further development of engraving techniques, cheap and affordable illustrated costume books became available throughout Europe, known in German as *Trachtenbucher*. These black-and-white pamphlets functioned as sartorial travel guides, showing how different cultures dressed and adorned themselves. People's natural curiosity made the engravings popular, and the exchange of different ideas about dress—who wore what and when and why—began to influence how people saw themselves. It was only a matter of time before someone made a journal specifically about fashion.

In 1672, the very first fashion magazine for men and women was published in France. Titled *Le Mercure galant* (The Gallant Mercury), it was published by Jean Donneau de Visé. The journal reported on not only fashion trends using engraved fashion illustrations, but also intellectual and artistic debates, marriage announcements, life in court, poems, songs, gossip, and news, as well as providing art and theater reviews. It was so successful that Louis XIV decreed that it be published monthly. Publication ended in 1674, but it later became a monthly under the name *Nouveau Mercure galant*. While the magazine played a significant role in disseminating French fashion among the elite, its impact among the general public was minimal; costume books were still more widely read. It wasn't until the mid-18th century, when the new hand-colored fashion plates arrived, that costume books suddenly became less desirable.

Fashion plates, unlike the old costume books, highlighted the latest style. These were the forerunners of contemporary fashion illustration and fashion design sketches. Fashion plates, typically depicting a clothed figure, drawn and engraved and later hand-colored, offered visual cues as to which fabric, accessory, or color was currently in vogue. Seen not only by consumers, but also by tailors and merchants, they became indispensable to anyone interested in fashion. They were so popular that they were not only included in pamphlets and books—and that new invention, the magazine—but also continued as an art form until the use of photography in the early 20th century. Still, a magazine devoted solely to men's fashion wouldn't arrive for another fifty years.

The first popular English men's publication was *The Gentleman's Magazine*. Published in 1731 by Edward Cave, it contained essays, poems, fiction, and politics, but no fashion or illustrations. It did, however, give us a new word: "magazine." Cave invented the word, supposedly derived from the Arabic word *makhazin*, meaning storehouse; it slipped into common usage thereafter.

However, it was the *Journal des Dames et des Modes*, a French fashion pamphlet created in 1797, that finally included fashion art, occasionally showcasing men along with women's fashion illustration. The journal signaled a new way of dressing. Taking its cue from the egalitarian spirit of the revolution, it rejected the former regime's rules for dressing that signaled one's social rank. Lavish embroidery, powdered wigs, extravagant lace, and colorful silk were gone; now men wore somber, tailored suits

and coats, hinting at the fashions to come. The journal ended in 1804, just before Napoleon became emperor, but was later revived in 1912.

It was during the Industrial Revolution, in the middle of the nineteenth century, that technological advances helped to create an audience for fashion illustration. A growing literate middle class with more purchasing power and the mass production of manufactured goods all led to the development of mass media. Businesses, including fashion houses and clothing manufacturers, responded with advertising. Newspapers, posters, pamphlets, and illustrated newspapers all competed for readership and advertising dollars. Gradually, promoting a product or garment through an advertisement became an important selling tool, and new visual aids—the rotary printing press, photography, illustration, and design sketches—became central to the dissemination of fashion art. Quite a few men's fashion illustrations at this time were of a high caliber, but many others were stiff and more than a little lifeless. This was because of the need to accurately convey the details of a garment, its construction, the texture of fabric, number of buttons, etc. These illustrations were functional and meant to be informative rather than expressive; this may have been due to the way fashion plates were made.

Creating a fashion plate during this period was a lot like creating a contemporary fashion illustration. An artist would first draw the clothed figure in pencil, often in some sort of environment—a garden or some interior; then, the engraver, who might be the artist, would engrave the drawing on a metal plate with sharp etching tools. Inks would be applied to the plate, a paper would be placed on top, and then a roller would be pressed and the drawing would be transferred to the paper. Once the paper was dry, an assembly line—usually women—would hand paint the engraving with watercolor or ink. Each person would be

Figure 1.3 Men's fashions, 1896, Library of Congress.

Figure 1.4 Leon Bonnette, Fashionable men in black, 1919. Science History Images / Alamy Stock Photo.

responsible for applying one color; it was a team effort. Sometimes, even a particular rendering would be parceled out: One artist might specialize in heads, another in backgrounds, and another artist might only focus on fabric details like tweed or plaids. Viewed this way, it is understandable why men's fashion art of this period was so rigid and uninspiring. There was little individuality.

While there were several magazines for men during this period with titles like *Man About Town*, *Gentleman's Pictorial*, and *Country Gentleman*, most of these closed in 1914 at the beginning of the First World War.

It was the birth of *Gazette du Bon Ton* in 1912 that signaled the beginning of men's fashion illustration as a genuine cultural force. Published by the Librairie Centrale des Beaux-Arts, with

Lucien Vogel as *directeur*, the expensive and exclusive journal combined the gossip of French high society with serious essays about fashion, art, and politics. It also introduced, through its beautifully illustrated pages, artists who would become famous just ten years later: artists such as Bernard Boutet de Monvel, Georges Lepape, Charles Martin, André Marty, Paul Iribe, Benito, Pierre Brissaud, and, in particular, George Barbier. Unlike the teams of anonymous technicians who had created fashion illustrations just fifty years earlier, these illustrators were allowed to complete an illustration from beginning to end. By the 1920s they would not only be inspired by the post-war years of fast cars, nightclubs, and flying machines, but also by the explosion of new fine art: the work of Matisse and his group of *Fauves*, or "Wild Beasts," the arrival of the Ballets Russes and the daring and innovative work of Léon Bakst, the influential exhibition of Japanese prints in the late 1880s, and, of course, Picasso's exploration of Cubism. The resulting effect was expressive and idiosyncratic works of art. While not every seam or button was documented, the overall impact was somehow stronger. It was during these early decades of the 20th century that fashion illustration became a profession. These artists—all trained at the great Parisian art school, the École des Beaux-Arts—helped to define what we now call Art Deco and helped lay the groundwork for what became the Golden Age of Fashion Illustration, after the First World War.

The Golden Age of Men's Fashion Illustration: 1919–39

The turn of the new century saw a flood of new lifestyle and fashion magazines, particularly in the United States. By 1900, there were no fewer than fifty US national fashion magazines, and these would, along with radio, provide advertisers with a means of mass communication. Magazines and illustrated newspapers were a cheap and easy form of entertainment. Advertisers hired illustrators to sell their products, and publishers hired illustrators to boost their sales and increase advertising revenue with captivating magazine covers. As the financial success of illustrated magazines took off, the need for commissioned artwork grew. This in turn created competition among art directors and publishers for the limited number of exceptional artists, and by the mid-1920s the list of well-known American illustrators became a who's who of iconic figures. A partial list includes Charles Dana Gibson, John Held, Jr., Russell Patterson, C. Coles Phillips, Dean Cornwell,

James Montgomery Flagg, the German illustrator Ernst Dryden, and Norman Rockwell. But only one illustrator seemed to successfully corner the market on men's fashion illustration: Joseph Christian Leyendecker.

J. C. Leyendecker (1874–1951) was one of America's most popular illustrators in the early decades of the 20th century. His advertising art for menswear companies like Arrow Collar—a brand of detachable shirt collars—The House of Kuppenheimer, Hart Schaffner Marx, and Interwoven Socks had an enormous impact on the public. In fact, it is difficult to imagine today the type of success Leyendecker had in the early 1900s. Just as Charles Dana Gibson had originated the prototype of the beautiful and elegant American "Gibson Girl," Leyendecker recreated the Dandy as a smartly dressed young American. With his gleaming, brushed back hair, prominent chin, and broad shoulders, he was a virile but elegant gentleman. Such illustrations of handsome and beautifully dressed men had the same glamorous appeal then that Hollywood stars such as Gary Cooper or Cary Grant would have later.

Born in Germany, but raised from the age of eight in Chicago, Leyendecker's early art education was typical of young artists of the late 19th century. At age sixteen, he apprenticed at an engraving house; after work, he attended evening drawing classes. Later, with support from his working-class family, he and his brother Frank—also a talented artist—studied art at the Académie Julian in Paris. Leyendecker's training was what we would now describe as "classical." He studied drawing from plaster casts and still life and made exact copies of classic paintings. Even as a student, he won renown as a master draftsman. The brothers returned to the United States in 1897 and soon embarked on successful careers as illustrators.

Figure 1.5 J. C. Leyendecker, Kuppenheimer suits, 1920s. Image Courtesy of The Advertising Archives.

By the early 1920s, Leyendecker's Arrow Man illustrations were receiving fan mail—including marriage proposals and gifts—by the thousands. The Arrow Man became the subject of poems, songs, and even a Broadway play. And all of this was due to Leyendecker's extraordinary talent. His men seemed to symbolize the sleekly decadent Jazz Age sensibility of the 1930s, while paradoxically still appearing wholesome and all-American, despite the often subtle gay subtext. Notwithstanding his superb fashion sense, Leyendecker was never just a fashion illustrator, and during the Depression, when he lost most of his fashion clients, he simply moved on to magazine covers. His covers for *The Post*, *Collier's*, and *The Saturday Evening Post*, to name a few, were seen by millions of readers and helped to make him a small fortune. During his prolific professional career, in addition to magazine covers, he painted book covers, advertisements, posters, and magazine illustrations. No less an expert illustrator than Norman Rockwell idolized him.

As one of the leading lights of America's Golden Age of Illustration, Leyendecker's work has seeped into our cultural memory. After several decades in which he seemed forgotten, he is enjoying a much-deserved rediscovery: His work helped to capture and define a particular type of fashionable man in the early years of the 20th century, and designers and illustrators have returned to this for inspiration again and again.

Successful fashion magazines not only reflect the times in which they exist but also forecast what is to come. They create a visual diary, recording the thoughts, desires, and imaginations of a particular society at a given time. There were several men's magazines in the 1920s that did just that, with a focus on fashion and illustrations: *Der Herr* in Germany and *Monsieur* (1920–2) and *L'Homme Elégant* in France, but in particular the American magazine *Apparel Arts*.

Apparel Arts was created in 1931 as a men's fashion magazine for the clothing trade: designers, wholesale merchandisers, tailors, and retail sellers. Because it was primarily a fashion guide for industry insiders, its publications, printed quarterly, were limited: Its purpose was as a fashion forecast guide. Unlike the stylized illustrations of the early 1920s, menswear illustration in the 1930s tended toward realism. Details such as the width of a lapel, or the drape of a pant, were faithfully recorded to suggest the precise construction of a garment. There were no menswear designers during this time, only tailors, so *Apparel Arts*'s aim was to show how certain fabrics, tailoring, and silhouettes could be worn, and thus sold. But from the beginning it was very popular with retail customers, in large part due to its fashion illustrations—and one only has to look at the illustrations to see the lure.

Figure 1.6 Golf men, *Apparel Arts*, 1940s. Image Courtesy of The Advertising Archives.

A stable of fine illustrators—some staff, some freelance—did the work; chief among them were Robert Goodman (1911–48), Leslie Saalburg (1897–1973), and Laurence Fellows (1885–1964). The works of these artists were more than just drawings of a model in a particular outfit; very often, the men's clothing painted in the illustrations was completely made up. First, artists were given a general theme; they would then imagine and create a detailed scene, with the model wearing the clothes in an appropriate environment. The typical *Apparel Arts* man was a mature, prosperous gentleman doing what prosperous gentlemen do: attending boardroom meetings, going to cocktail parties, visiting nightclubs, sailing, golfing, etc. Expertly rendered in vibrant watercolor with confident brushstrokes, carefully delineated shapes, subtle shadows, and an economy of line, the illustrated *Apparel Arts* man came to vivid life as a sophisticated and urbane man of means. To view these illustrations now is to see a striking evocation of the 1930s and early 1940s: an era of elegant tuxedos, rakish Fedoras, and perfumed boutonnieres.

In 1933, the popularity of *Apparel Arts* led to the creation of the first men's magazine in the United States: *Esquire* magazine. Unlike most men's magazines, this one was focused on fashion. By 1957, *Apparel Arts*, still published by *Esquire*, was transformed back into a quarterly magazine. A year later, the magazine was renamed *Gentleman's Quarterly* and made a monthly periodical. The magazine was rebranded yet again, in 1967, as *GQ*.

From 1939 to 1945, menswear fashion trends were forced to take a back seat to war; Second World War military uniforms were almost universal for men in Europe and North America. Those not in uniform wore a suit not too different from that of the 1930s: broad-shouldered suits, single- or double-breasted, wide, pleated pants worn above the waist, polished shoes, and a Fedora. Flash was out, sobriety was in. Fashion illustration was still seen in national retail advertisements in newspapers and magazines, but editorial fashion art spreads disappeared. Even *Apparel Arts* stopped showing men's fashion art.

The Post-War Years: 1945–60

The post-war years began as a slow continuation of the late 1930s, minus the optimism. The war may have ended, but there were still major shortages: With European economies shattered, necessities were still being rationed. It wasn't until the late 1940s that a semblance of normalcy returned. With aid from the United States in the form of the Marshall Plan and government rebuilding, people began to buy things again. A consumerist society started to develop, influenced by US cultural and political power. Christian Dior's "New Look," in 1947, marked a new age in women's fashion, but there was no male equivalent, just a subtle change in the proportion and detail of the average man's suit and the introduction of synthetic fabrics. Radical change wouldn't occur until the 1960s. Instead of lavishly illustrated fashion editorials in men's magazines, fashion illustrations were only advertising basic and mundane menswear, like flannel shirts and overcoats. Fashion illustration had begun a slow but steady decline.

Nevertheless, editorial fashion art had a brief reprieve in the mid-1950s. There were many fine commercial artists, but few who specialized in men's fashion illustration; the few who did made a name for themselves. Some of the international artists whose work helped to define fashion art in that decade include Gerd Grimm (1911–98) in Germany, Eric Stemp (1924–2001) and Brian Stonehouse (1918–98) in the UK, Max Hoff

Figure 1.7 Cover of *Sir*—René Gruau. © The Advertising Archives / Bridgeman Images.

(born Maximilian J. A. Hofbauer, 1903–85) in Austria, and the Japanese artist Setsu Nagasawa (1917–99). Though all were brilliant and successful, none had the popularity or longevity of France's René Gruau.

Gruau (1909–2004) was a fashion illustrator of remarkable skill and style. His glamorous illustrations, particularly for Christian Dior during the post-Second World War years, exemplified the restored elegance of Parisian fashion. Born in Rimini, Italy, in 1910 as Count Renato Zavagli Ricciardelli, he took his mother's maiden name, Gruau, after his parents' separation and divorce, and was first published at the age of fifteen, after moving to Paris with his mother. For much of the 1930s he worked for fashion magazines and advertising agencies; Gruau later said he

found work scarce during the war years. Later, in the 1940s and 1950s, he worked with French couturiers Jacques Fath, Pierre Balmain, and Hubert de Givenchy, but he was most closely associated with Dior. His illustrations in watercolor and gouache displayed a bold graphic sense often highlighted with a sinuous black line, revealing the influences of Toulouse-Lautrec and Japanese calligraphy. The Gruau man was a lean and elegant creation, a European gentleman at ease in black tie and self-assured in a pinstriped suit. Gruau's menswear images share the same mode of expression as his women's fashion art: complex but sparing illustrations with a strong graphic sense, and with just enough imagery to suggest an environment or narrative. While he continued working until his death at the age of ninety-five, his most influential period as a commercial artist was in the 1950s and 1960s.

The Silver Age of Men's Fashion Illustration: 1960–89

Whenever anyone mentions the 1960s, the first things that usually come to mind are miniskirts, long hair, love beads, and the Beatles. Obviously, the 1960s amounted to much more than that. And one way to view the decade, or any decade for that matter, is to remember that decades are artificial measurements of time. The 1950s didn't end precisely at midnight on December 31, 1959, and the 1960s didn't disappear at 12:01 a.m. on January 1, 1970. In fact, one could argue that there were three distinct fashion periods in the 1960s, and the first third of the decade was a continuation of the late 1950s establishment look.

Leaving aside the growing phenomenon of US sportswear, the early 1960s men's suit was a leaner, trimmer silhouette. Think of the sober, shapeless suit worn by Gregory Peck in *The Man in the Gray Flannel Suit*, a 1956 film about the corporate conformity of the 1950s. Now,' recall the sleekly tailored Sean Connery as James Bond in 1964's *Goldfinger*. This is the menswear look of the early 1960s. The sophisticated and mature man of the 1930s *Apparel Arts* became a younger, more athletic, but still cosmopolitan, gentleman: This is made clear in the illustrations of Al Pimsler.

Alvin J. Pimsler (1918–2014) was born in Flushing, New York. He graduated from the Pratt Institute School of Fine and Applied Arts in 1938. In 1941 he was drafted into the army and became a first lieutenant. While overseas, he was later captured and became a prisoner of war (POW). With the fall of Berlin in 1945, POW camps were swiftly abandoned by German soldiers, and Pimsler soon escaped with other POWs. Weeks later, he and others were found by US forces and shipped back to the States. After returning from the war, Pimsler married, had children, and spent the next several decades establishing himself as a distinguished and influential fashion illustrator. Pimsler's illustrations were like him: handsome and urbane, but also graphic and dynamic. His work, like those of his fellow illustrators of the period—Marbury Brown, Bob Peak, Jim Dickerson, Harlan Krakowitz, and Austin Briggs—responded to the competitive challenge of fashion photography by reducing a fashion drawing to its bare essential: line. Using a thick charcoal stub, a thin graphite pencil, or a chiseled black marker, Pimsler stripped away anything that might compete with the energetic and descriptive line of a drawing. He worked often with models, drawing directly from them with pencils and watercolor washes, giving his illustrations a spontaneity and forcefulness that contrasted dramatically with the fashion

photographs of the day. Pimsler continued to work as an illustrator through several decades, teaching at several art colleges, and later becoming the president of the Society of Illustrators in New York. He died at the age of ninety-six.

The 1960s and 1970s were dizzying and tumultuous decades. The status quo was being challenged as never before: from the black civil rights movement to the Vietnam War protests, from the gay liberation struggle to the feminist movement. Serious artists of all stripes responded to this rapid social change in a variety of ways, but few fashion illustrators were as representative of the period as Antonio Lopez. He managed, with remarkable virtuosity, to redefine and reinvigorate fashion illustration even as the profession was dying. While he was not the first illustrator known for his versatility, he was the first to aggressively adapt his style to the ever-changing 1960s, 1970s, and 1980s. And his extraordinary visual vocabulary, along with his graphic and decorative boldness, seemed to not only reflect those times, but to also predict the future of both fashion and art. It is this remarkable adaptability that may have made it possible for him to succeed where others had failed, even though fashion illustration had been on a slow decline since the early 1960s.

Antonio was blessed with many gifts; one of many was his exquisite sense of timing. Born in 1943, in Utuado, Puerto Rico, he came of age as an illustrator in 1963, when fashion illustration was at its lowest ebb. By age two, he was drawing pictures of his mother, a seamstress and dressmaker. In his early teens he was a student at the Fashion Institute of Technology (FIT) in New York, and it was there that he met his life-long friend and associate, Juan Eugene Ramos (1942–95). Juan became his creative collaborator, sometime office manager, researcher, and

Figure 1.8 Business Group—Alvin Pimsler. Images courtesy of
Fashion Institute of Technology SUNY FIT Library of Special
Collections and College Archives.

sounding board. Though their romantic relationship ended after several years, it was Juan, through his own considerable artistic instincts and knowledge, who channeled and directed Antonio's creative impulses. It was Juan who could criticize Antonio's work and demand changes and make sure they happened. And it was Juan who was with Antonio at the end. Although their long association was sometimes challenging, both recognized how essential their teamwork was to their success. At nineteen, Antonio dropped out of FIT when offered a job at *Women's Wear Daily*. After six months, he left to accept a position at the *New York Times*. And it was here that Antonio's career began its spectacular ascent.

While his earlier work was reminiscent of René Bouché and Kenneth Paul Block—elegant charcoal renderings of fashionably sedate women—he now carved out a different path. Unlike older fashion illustrators, who tended to glamorize and invent the upper classes, Antonio's work, like that of so many commercial and fine artists of the period, reflected a new idealization of youth. Former social and cultural standards were breaking down. The old guard was dead.

Antonio had always worked from life. In fact, his use of friends and acquaintances as models was a continuous source of inspiration—a defining aspect of his art that will be discussed later—as he began to experiment with different media and concepts. And in this he was encouraged by a kindred spirit, Katharina Denzinger (1931–2019). Denzinger was a German-born fashion illustrator and friend of Antonio's, best known for her avant-garde fashion illustrations in *Harper's Bazaar* and for her collaborative work with Richard Avedon. She, like Antonio, believed that rather than just putting a figure down on paper, one should think about the narrative or graphic concept behind the piece, and let the

viewer intuit the story or theme. Rather than stay in one commercial style, why not learn and borrow from Boldini or Léger? This constant need to reimagine the style of his work, and the methods that went with it, not only became Antonio's signature, but also allowed him to stay one step ahead of the crowd. His experiments with different media seemed a never-ending process: color pencils, markers, gouache, watercolor, collage, inks, colored film, photomontage, computer-generated images—all were used and explored. His artistic influences were legion—Warhol, Hockney, Rauschenberg, Baskt, dance, music, Japanese prints, film, and photo realism, to name but a few—but this referencing of contemporary fine art would be his most consistent influence. He was like an all-seeing and omnivorous fashion editor who just happened to be a superb draftsman. If there was one singular difference in Antonio's approach to fashion illustration, it was his use of what were then considered unconventional models.

For most of the 20th century, the ideal man, and therefore the ideal man of fashion, was tall, mature, wealthy, white, and straight. As mentioned earlier, the 1960s, 1970s, and 1980s were decades in which the values and social structures were constantly being challenged. Therefore, it came as little surprise to see these changes reflected in popular culture. However, to see these developments in fashion illustration was, at the time, revolutionary. Antonio's drawings of black, Asian, Latino, and gay men (his friends and acquaintances) echoed the contemporary—and still relevant—discussion of what constituted a "fashionable man." His enthusiastic embrace of those normally rejected by fashion professionals as not only beautiful, but also glamorous, contributed to a redefinition of what is beautiful today. It's doubtful that Antonio was

Figure 1.9 Antonio—Personal study, Mike Morino. 1983, pencil, watercolor, and gold paint on paper. The Estate & Archives of Antonio Lopez and Juan Ramos.

heavily involved in any intellectual critique concerning ideas regarding dress, masculinity, race, or gender representation. But he didn't have to be—his art itself did that for him.

Antonio's prolific career sent him to Paris, where he and Juan spent seven years. Later, he traveled to the major fashion capitals of the world, bringing his exciting and eclectic view of fashion with him. By the late 1970s he and Juan had returned to New York and settled in a loft on Union Square West. There, his studio became a major meeting place for artists, models, dancers, and anyone one else who amused or interested the couple. During this time, his work included illustrations for designers, advertising campaigns for department stores, album covers, lectures, and portraits. He worked closely with Anna Piaggi on the magazine *Vanity*, and later published two books, *Antonio's Girls* and *Antonio's Tales of 1001 Nights*. He was the only artist to be regularly featured in *Vogue*.

Antonio Lopez died in Los Angeles in 1987; he was forty-four. His long-time friend and collaborator, Juan Ramos, died in 1995; he was fifty-three. Both died of AIDS. Antonio's ceaseless exploration and redefinition of fashion illustration was, and is, widely applauded, and continues to influence fashion artists to this day.

By the mid-1980s fashion illustration was rarely seen in men's magazines; there were popular and influential fashion artists like Tony Viramontes, but no one illustrator dominated menswear illustration: Photography had long supplanted illustration as the dominant producer of men's fashion images. And yet one could still find, here and there, examples of menswear art. There were advertisements in New York department stores like Bloomingdales, Lord & Taylor, and Barney's. At Bergdorf Goodman, George Stavrinos produced exquisitely drawn fashion illustrations that recalled the academic drawings of John Singer Sargent. Editorial spreads with fashion illustrations occasionally appeared in art magazines like *La Mode en peinture* (1982), Condé Nast's *Vanity* (1981), and *Visionaire* (1991). Lastly, there were the fashion trade magazines like *L'Officiel de la mode et du couture*, *International Textiles*, and *Sir*, which continued to inform the merchandisers, designers, and fabric houses that made up the fashion insiders. In New York the menswear trade magazine of choice was *DNR*.

The *Daily News Record* (or *DNR*) was an American trade journal that specialized in men's fashion. Created in 1890 by Edmund Fairchild, it began as a mimeograph paper, then called the *Daily Trade Record*, and was distributed at the Chicago World's Fair in 1893. The paper proved so popular that Fairchild and his brother Luis decided to continue publishing the paper after the fair was over. The journal became known as the *Daily News Record* in 1916. Later, a small section devoted to women's wear was added to the paper. Soon this feature would split from the journal and be given its own publication, titled *Women's Wear Daily* (*WWD*). In 1960, John Fairchild changed the look of *WWD* and *DNR* by employing a team of talented illustrators to provide up-to-the-minute coverage of the fast-changing fashion market. Unusually for their time, *WWD* and *DNR* allowed artists (often fully credited) almost complete freedom to record and interpret the zeitgeist as they saw it. These staff illustrators worked for a daily trade paper with almost impossible deadlines, yet their initial creative impulses helped to shape how many readers perceived current fashion. A partial list of these incredible artists includes Kenneth Paul Block, Steven Stipelman, Antonio, Pedro Barrios, Steven Meisel, Catherine Clayton Purnell, Anneliese Gmelch, Richard

Rosenfeld, Glenn Tunstull, Robert Passantino, Kichisaburo Ogawa, and Robert Melendez. Melendez would eventually become the signature artist for *DNR*.

Robert Melendez (1944–) was born in Ybor City, a neighborhood in Tampa, Florida, the youngest of five children. His parents, both from Puerto Rico, had moved to Tampa in the mid-1920s. Inspired by an older sister, the popular Katy Keene comics, and illustrated department store ads, Melendez became interested in fashion illustration. Once he was accepted to Parsons School of Design, Melendez left Florida for New York. As a student, he worked his way through college, and on the recommendation of one of his instructors, Anneliese Gmelch, he was hired to work at *WWD* three days a week during his

Figure 1.10 *DNR* cover 1979—Robert Melendez. Images courtesy of Fashion Institute of Technology SUNY FIT Library of Special Collections and College Archives.

final semester, before graduation. Melendez was hired as a full-time staff artist in June 1967. His association with *WWD* and *DNR* would last nearly a quarter century. Like any professional illustrator who manages to work for decades, Melendez was extremely versatile. Inspired by popular culture, fine art, and classic fashion illustration, he was constantly reinventing his approach to fashion art. He worked in Rapidograph pen for line drawings, color pencils, charcoal, watercolor, markers, airbrush, and color adhesive film, perfecting each style. Melendez's hard-edged layouts and bold graphic figures were reflections of 1980s New Wave, and the Milanese Memphis Group. These post-modern art movements, a blended style of Art Deco, Pop Art, and the kitsch styles of the 1950s, can be seen in some of the art of the decade along with some of Melendez's color illustrations. Working from life and from reference files for inspiration, his menswear illustrations are cool, colorful, and graphic. Although highly stylized, with precise black lines and ellipses reminiscent of architectural drawings, his beautifully rendered men still come across as recognizable types. With their broad padded shoulders and dimpled chins, Melendez's men are often sexy and always fashionable. His *DNR* art constantly showcases abstraction and asymmetry, but never loses sight of the figure, or the clothes he's tasked with illustrating. His compositions and layouts always manage to effortlessly enhance his figures. Melendez left *DNR* in the late 1980s and rejoined *WWD*. He left a few years later, when photography replaced illustrations at *WWD*, and became a freelance artist at Simplicity Pattern Company specializing in graphic design and digital art. He retired in 2017.

In 1999, Fairchild Publications, Inc. was sold to Condé Nast Publications after being briefly owned by The Walt Disney Company. *DNR*'s print edition ended in 2008, and its men's fashion coverage was absorbed into *WWD*. It is now an online-only publication.

Men's Fashion Illustration Today: 1990–

The last two decades of the 20th century, and the first two decades of the 21st, were interesting times for fashion illustration precisely because the changes to the profession seemed so contradictory. On the one hand, fashion illustration in general, and men's fashion illustration in particular, was in obvious decline: Editorial fashion illustrations in magazines were increasingly rare, and the type of retail advertising art that was once popular in daily newspapers was slowly disappearing. On the other hand, there was an explosion of new and original talent that seemed to defy the early death notices for fashion illustration. By the mid-1990s artists of all stripes were experimenting with various digital programs such as Photoshop and Illustrator. The availability and freedom of this new medium led to online media and the creation of blogs, websites, and digital magazines; this in turn led to artists attempting new ways of illustrating for online and print publications.

For fashion designers, the computer became a design tool, another way to explain and enhance a designer's ideas. For illustrators, fashion illustration seemed to morph from a profession solely focused on fashion to one that redefined itself as "lifestyle" illustration. This small effort at rebranding helped to broaden the ways in which a fashion illustrator could, depending on their skill and tenacity, compete in some small way with general illustrators. The work of these new illustrators was so varied and original that

they managed to remind art directors and fashion editors just how compelling fashion art could be. Fashion illustrators such as Colin Barnes, Thierry Perez, Gladys Perint Palmer, Jason Brooks, Stefano Canulli, Ruben Toledo, Jordi Labanda, Lorenzo Mattotti, Jean-Philippe Delhomme, François Berthoud, Kareem Iliya, and, in particular, Mats Gustafson and David Downton reconceived modern fashion illustration, thereby making it relevant again. Most of these artists specialized in women's fashion illustration, but there were those who also had a feeling for men's fashion; Eduard Erlikh was one of them.

Erlikh's watercolor drawings are fluid shadows, vivid and colorful figures that seem to prance and spin on an invisible catwalk. While his dynamic silhouettes sometimes lack the details of more realistic fashion drawings, they more than

Figure 1.11 Orange Trench—Eduard Erlikh.

make up for this in their movement and attitude. His men are, in a word, hip. Eduard Erlikh was born in Russia, in 1962. He attended the Art Academy in Moscow from the age of eight. At sixteen, he studied fashion and costume design at the Moscow Textile Institute, and at twenty he studied fashion illustration in New York, at the FIT and Parsons School of Design. His big break came when the US *Vogue* magazine called him to illustrate a massive 24-page ad campaign. From there he went on to create ad campaigns for Tiffany & Co., Lanvin, Ann Taylor, Clinique, and Cinzano, along with editorial work for *Elle*, *Bazaar*, *Madame Figaro*, and *L'Officiel*, to name a few. He has also designed costumes for ballet and has had his work exhibited by the Vienna State Opera Museum. Erlikh's illustrations, like many of his contemporaries', deal with abstraction. He does not draw faces or fingers and appears less concerned with an exact representation of a fashion model than with his idea of how a garment would actually look on a moving figure. Rendered in bright, flamboyant colors, his swaggering men seem animated by club music that only they can hear. Erlikh's men are that rare thing in fashion illustration: they are sexy. The world is their runway. Despite his emphatic modernity, Erlikh's vivid and exuberant watercolor paintings share the same flowing lines and graphic shapes as earlier fashion artists like Christian Bérard and Marcel Vertès.

PHOTOGRAPHY VS. ILLUSTRATION

One of the more persuasive explanations for the popularity of photography over fashion illustration is the belief that a photograph simply records reality—the viewer often conveniently ignoring the person behind the camera—while a drawing is a subjective interpretation of a subject.

Despite what we know about Photoshop and computer-generated images, many people believe photography is a more honest and reliable image conveyor, regardless of how faithful or realistic an artist's rendering of a subject might be. Illustrators' reactions to the pervasiveness of photography have varied. Some ignore the rivalry, while others (e.g., Andy Warhol) abandon fashion illustration for another field. A select few rise to the challenge head-on. One such artist is Richard Kilroy.

British-born illustrator Richard Kilroy grew up obsessively drawing cartoon and video-game characters. In his teens, he discovered fashion illustration through the Art Nouveau posters of Alphonse Mucha, and the occasional fashion art of *The Face* magazine. After graduating from Leeds College of Art, he began his career

Figure 1.12 Richard Kilroy—Lanvin 12.

as a fashion illustrator, concentrating on menswear. His work includes editorial illustrations for *VMan*, *Homme Style*, and *Numero* magazines, and work for Canali, Paul Smith, Christian Dior, and Elton John.

Kilroy's incisive drawings subtly mimic photography while being clearly handmade. Using a graphite pencil to skillfully render a face, an arm, or a suit jacket, Kilroy can capture the stillness and detailed appearance of a photograph while also making brushstrokes and pencil marks that are emphatically man-made. Blending photorealism, negative space, and color blocking with simple lines, he is able to produce extraordinary work that is both a commentary on the collision between illustration and photography, and a unique take on menswear illustration. His work continues to develop, and his subject matter has expanded. In 2015, Kilroy wrote *Menswear Illustration*, one of the rare books on contemporary men's fashion illustration.

There is no longer a common artistic look or feel among current menswear illustrators. Today, unlike in decades past, there is no single dominant style. This freedom allows artists who concentrate on menswear to approach the subject with different emphases, some using a particular medium to convey their vision, others changing their approach to men's fashion illustration as often as their mood or clients demand. The work of Carlos Aponte is a prime example of the latter. Aponte works in a variety of illustrative styles, but each one exhibits a strong graphic sense and an unerring eye for shape and line.

Carlos Aponte was born in New York and raised in Puerto Rico. While in school, a favorite teacher encouraged him to become a fashion designer, and after graduating high school and winning a scholarship, he attended Parsons School of Design as a fashion design major. He returned to Puerto Rico two years later and became a designer for a local design house. It was while working as a designer that he attended a major fashion event in San Juan, and it was there that he met Antonio Lopez. Though more of a warm acquaintance than a close friendship, Aponte's relationship with Antonio was nevertheless life-altering. Two years later, he would return to New York, with Antonio's encouragement, and attend FIT and the School of Visual Arts. Aponte first gained widespread notice as a menswear illustrator with his masking-tape illustrations for *Visionaire* magazine; his bold, abstracted images were an imaginative new take on men's fashion illustration. Witty, original, and somewhat ominous, his masking-tape art was also exquisitely drawn, and it is this skill as a draftsman that is apparent in all of his subsequent work. The clean, varied lines of his marker drawings, or the digital figures that mimic chalk renderings, are the result of disciplined observation and skill. Influenced by Antonio and the fashion artist Jack Potter, Aponte's art has an elegant simplicity that resists becoming merely decorative. His minimalist illustrations are an expressive distillation of whatever his subject is, whether it is a walking figure, a man in a hat, or a cathedral. Aponte's work has been featured in the *New York Times*, *Elle* and *Esquire* magazines, Bil Donovan's *Advanced Fashion Illustration*, and Richard Kilroy's *Menswear Illustration*.

We are inundated by images—we can't escape them. We see them on our smartphones, on our TV screens, in movie theaters, in magazines, and on websites. And most of these images are photographs. Our visual expectations have been conditioned by photographic and computer-generated images of what we see every

Figure 1.13 Lanvin 6—(Tape Figure) Carlos Aponte.

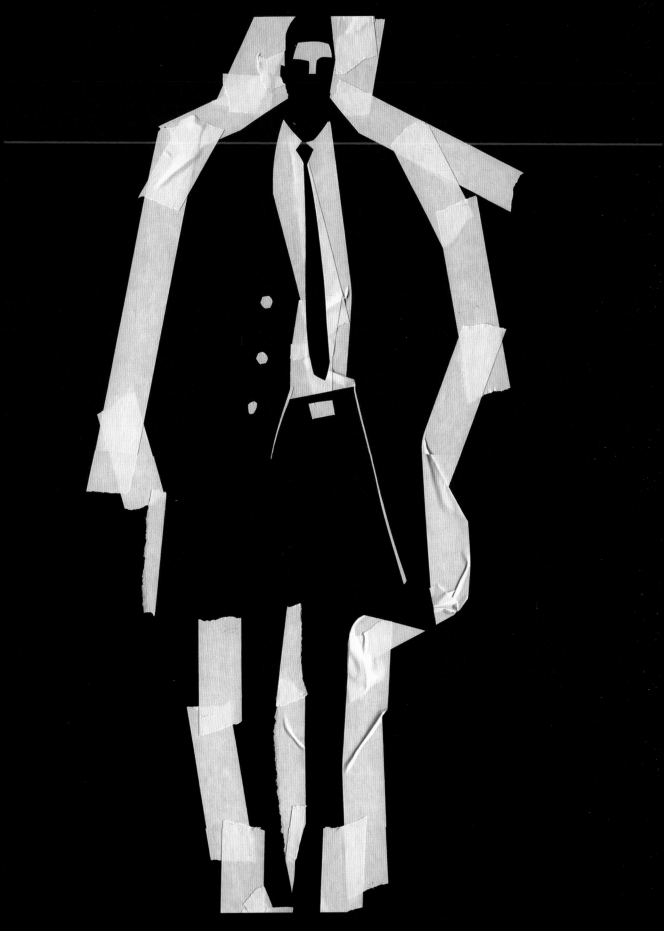

day. The photograph has become the dominant form of image representation today. Small wonder, then, that many illustrators choose to emphasize the comparison between the camera and the artist, by either further exploring our contemporary interest in abstraction or choosing to highlight the contrast by reaching farther back, to the academic and classical tradition of earlier artists. Ryan McMenamy is such an illustrator.

McMenamy, who lives in New York, creates work that is beautifully and unambiguously hand-drawn. Charcoaled figures are either appealingly rendered in chiaroscuro, with dark patches of background that throw into relief the highlighted folds of a garment, or they are painted, and cropped figures are done in flat planes of color. He is influenced by John Singer Sargent, Edward Hopper, and every Wyeth (N. C., Andrew, and Jamie), artists whose work reflects his love of the academic training of the late 19th and early 20th centuries. Yet his art is anything but old-fashioned. McMenamy was born in Duxbury, Massachusetts. He attended Parsons School of Design with the intent of becoming a fashion designer. However, during his foundation year he discovered how much he loved drawing, and soon switched his major to Illustration, eventually graduating with a Master of Fine Arts. McMenamy's art consists of abbreviated narratives, and partial images, of fashionable men frozen in time. His cropped menswear figures, glamorous and opaque, are elegant shadows caught in a moment of action: leaning over a desk, putting on a coat, or crossing their legs while enjoying a drink. They hide behind sunglasses and hoodies, often turning their backs to the viewer. His men are handsome but mysterious, conservative but fashionable. His expertly drawn and edited scenes, with their positive and negative shapes, and his sparing graphic compositions may remind

Figure 1.14 Blue-suited man seated in a lounge. Artwork by Ryan McMenamy.

one of the posters of Toulouse-Lautrec and René Gruau. McMenamy's commercial clients include Calvin Klein, Bergdorf Goodman, *VMan*, *Men's File*, *Man of the World*, and H&M.

ILLUSTRATION IN THE AGE OF SOCIAL MEDIA

Globalization and social media have meant not only that images are instantly dispersed throughout the world, but also that new information platforms have developed in order to showcase these digital images. In the past, designers would have a collection photographed by a freelance photographer and then published in a trade paper, or magazine, usually in a few months. Now, such images are disseminated throughout the world almost instantly. And with this new rapidity, and the interest in online shows, there has been a return to fashion illustration as a form of reportage. Social media records these experiences and shares them with millions, all while imposing a narrative or story through pictures. By digitally illustrating backstage scenes, along with the models and the clothes, the artist can document the creative process with a unique and subjective eye and share the images almost instantaneously. And if the artist can do this with the skill and talent of an experienced illustrator, so much the better. That is the approach of George Gozum.

George Gozum's fashion art is distinguished by old-school draftsmanship and 21st-century computer skills; his distinctive works appear to be traditionally created by watercolor or pencil, but they are entirely digitally created. Gozum was born in Manila, in the Philippines. After graduating from an all-boys Catholic school, he attended the University of the Philippines and its College of Fine Arts, majoring in Visual

Communications. Gozum had always loved to draw, but believed his real strength was as a graphic designer. He spent the next several years traveling back and forth between New York and the Philippines, working as a menswear designer for a small men's boutique, a freelance art director, and finally, a creative director in New York for DG Williams, a top mannequin company. In 2011, after sitting in a class given by illustrator Bil Donovan, he decided to become a menswear illustrator. A year later, Gozum started a project where he would go backstage at several New York menswear fashion shows, and unasked, create old-school fashion reportage.

Fortuitously, that year was viewed by many as the beginning of a menswear renaissance, and Gozum, with his background as a designer and his skill as an artist, was able to stand out. This led to several young designers asking him to sketch their shows. The powerful images he created were used on social media and, not surprisingly, gained attention. Gozum's work is a unique blend of sophisticated software, superior draftsmanship, and a keen understanding of menswear. He works digitally, but the look of his art varies: One piece might look like an ink brush drawing, while another might look like a charcoal sketch—such is his skill. While he draws constantly from life, his finished online drawings always begin digitally. He does not scan his drawings, like many digital artists; instead, he uses the computer to make his images look as hand-drawn as possible. Gozum consciously mimics traditional media, mixing both classical and digital techniques, with one informing the other. His client list includes designers SIKI IM, Robert Geller, Antonio Azzuolo, Patrik Ervell, Sony, and Amazon. However, George Gozum is not the only illustrator involved in fashion reportage; he shares that distinction with another artist, Richard Haines.

Figure 1.15 Image courtesy of George Gozum.

HAINES

Figure 1.16 Richard Haines—Thom Browne, *25 percent*.

Richard Haines is one of the most in-demand menswear artists in the field today. His ubiquitous charcoal drawings of fashionable men have been in magazines, catalogs, and books, and on window displays and clothing around the world. He has collaborated and worked with designers such as Dries Van Noten and Miuccia Prada, and yet his career as a menswear artist began rather late in life. Haines was born in Panama but raised in Idaho. Like many artists, he started sketching at a young age, drawing gardens and bridal gowns as a way of coping with the illness of his father. As he got older, he copied the fashion illustrations he saw in newspapers. After graduating from high school in Washington, D.C., he attended Virginia Commonwealth University, where he majored in fine arts and graphic design. After graduation, Haines's first job was at Vogue Patterns as an assistant illustrator, sketching women's fashions. After leaving Vogue Patterns, he began a successful career as a menswear designer for Calvin Klein, Perry Ellis, Bill Blass, and Sean "Puffy" Combs. His abrupt change of careers occurred during the financial crash of 2008: It was then that he lost his job and apartment and moved to a loft in Brooklyn. There, he started a blog titled "What I Saw Today," using it to publicize his fashion illustrations. His blog eventually caught the eye of Miuccia Prada, who commissioned him to create illustrations for a line of T-shirts and a book. This highly sought commission took off and helped to establish Haines as a popular menswear artist. Since then, he has collaborated not only with Prada and Van Noten, but also with J. Crew, Oliver Peoples, and Valentino Haute Couture. Haines has also illustrated for the *New York Times*, *Paper Magazine*, *GQ*, *New York*, and *InStyle* magazines, and in 2019 Haines exhibited his work at the Daniel Cooney Gallery in New York. Frequently working from life, he sketches people, often unobtrusively, in parks, sidewalks, and subways. His effortlessly stylish men are hip and modern, but also flesh and blood. They don't pose, but instead stand relaxed and unselfconscious. His incisive and compelling drawings, like all good fashion art, describe for us the man, the place, and the time in a few spare lines. Haines works chiefly in charcoal, pastels, watercolor, and inks. His idiosyncratic, loose lines are fast, gestural, and kinetic. His appealing drawings manage to zero in on the salient details of the garment, while also conveying the look and mood of the model. He may repeat a line for emphasis, but his shapes are clear and evocative, leaving just enough unsaid to engage the viewer to complete the picture.

Fashion illustration has always existed in one form or another. The need to recreate a striking figure of fashion in paint, pencil, or digitally seems too strong to resist. And while traditionally most of the attention has focused on women's fashion illustration, the interest in menswear art has grown as men have become ever larger consumers of fashion. The history recounted here, while brief, is the story of some of the brilliant artists who, through their individual talents, have shaped the way we view the illustrated men of fashion of both the past and present.

New Common Projects
shoe collaboration

Robert adjusts the
pants fit

Robert Geller
contemplating
looks between
shots

neoprene
leggings!

Stylist
Yuji Takenaka

Behind the scenes:
Robert Geller SS13 Lookbook shoot 8/13/12

2

Drawing the Male Fashion Figure

What Makes a Good Fashion Drawing?

A good fashion drawing is both an idealized impression of a garment and an accurate statement of how the clothes should look on a figure. It can be a simple sketch of a few lines showing how a garment must be made, or a detailed illustration with a narrative structure and a formal composition. The individual decides the choice of style and medium. What is the artist or designer trying to say, and how do they say it? Is the sketch a problem-solving exercise, or a finished illustration for presentation? Since fashion art deals with a degree of fantasy, strict adherence to reality isn't necessary. It is up to the designer or illustrator to decide the look of the figures: Should they be highly stylized or realistic? Computer generated or hand-drawn? All art is a form of description,

so how do you say, in line and color, what *you* mean to say? What other creative choices must be made? This is where style comes in.

Style, in a fashion illustration, is a distinctive way of drawing or painting. It is a signature brushstroke, a particular graphic sense, or a characteristic way with line or color. But it is more than that: A design sketch must also have an individual approach to fashion. That might include stylized proportions, or artwork that is less realistic and more experimental. Most creative people have an aesthetic point of view, a consistent list of likes and dislikes. Your "style" is made up of your skill set, your changing strengths and weaknesses, your personal preferences, your artistic influences, and your evolution as a person and an artist. Style is the result of saying what you mean to say in a way that is appropriate to you and your medium. That your point of view of fashion will gradually be transferred into your artwork is not only inevitable but also expected. *Your* style is what separates you from another

Figure 2.1 Fashion Illustration George Gozum.

designer or artist. It is not only an expression of your individual aesthetic, but also your brand. Once you gain more experience and confidence, you will develop and refine your own style.

Because of the transitory nature of fashion, changes in the look of your drawings will occur over time. If you understand the fundamentals of fashion drawing—anatomy, balance, proportion, a rudimentary understanding of how clothes are made, and a familiarity with a variety of rendering techniques—you may alter your style to suit the current fashion. A good fashion drawing not only has a figure that effectively captures the essence of a garment, real or imagined, but also reflects the time and culture in which the garment was worn.

What Is the Difference between a Design Sketch and a Fashion Illustration?

A fashion design sketch is often like a television commercial in that it must tell the story of the garment at a glance—its construction, fit, fabric, and silhouette. It can be a detailed and realistic digital drawing or an impressionistic marker sketch, but brevity is everything. A good design sketch describes a fashion design with speed, clarity, and style. A fashion illustration is more like a movie: There is more time to flesh out the story. One might add more characters, create an environment, or develop a narrative, but the focus is on the man wearing the garment, and how he looks in it. A good fashion illustration is meant to capture the zeitgeist of the moment. It is not concerned with a literal explanation of the construction of the garment. Its aim is to evoke a spirit, and because its primary aim is to sell, it is meant to seduce. Both the designer's sketch and the fashion illustration

Figure 2.2 Renaldo Barnette—Design sketch.

Figure 2.3 Lamont O'Neal—cropped peacoat.

must explain and persuade, but to do so one must develop one's drawing ability. Drawing is a skill, and like all skills it must be learned. We learn to draw by drawing, drawing, and drawing some more. Illustrations communicate what is in the designer's head. The more practiced the drawing, the more articulate the design will be.

Proportion

For beginners, one of the most difficult concepts to grasp is the fashion proportion. It is not hard to understand why: It can be challenging enough to accurately draw a human figure, so to then proceed to stylize it to conform to an ideal body type would appear to be a further hurdle. But it really isn't as difficult as it sounds. The ancient Greeks developed a set of proportions for their idealized figures of gods and goddesses, and later, many artists such as Ingres, Michelangelo, Modigliani, and El Greco often created elongated figures to express emotion or to provide tension within a composition. Every culture has created its own version of the physical ideal, though, inevitably, that archetype changes over time. Proportions change when fashion ideals change. In fashion illustration, the figure was habitually stretched to be slimmer and more graceful, to be in accordance with current aesthetic norms; consequently, a thinner, taller figure afforded more space for the garment to be shown. Nevertheless, one would be remiss to ignore the fashion world's increasing acknowledgment and representation of diverse body types. Many designers are responding to consumer demand and including body types that have long been ignored. Today, there are clothes for very tall or short men, plus-sized or full-figured men. Designers are also creating adaptive clothing for seniors and people with disabilities. Recently, gender-fluid and

Figure 2.4 Parke & Ronen Spring 2018 show. Photo by JP Yim/Getty Images for Parke & Ronen.

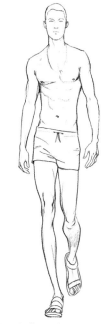

Figure 2.5 Swimsuit illustration.

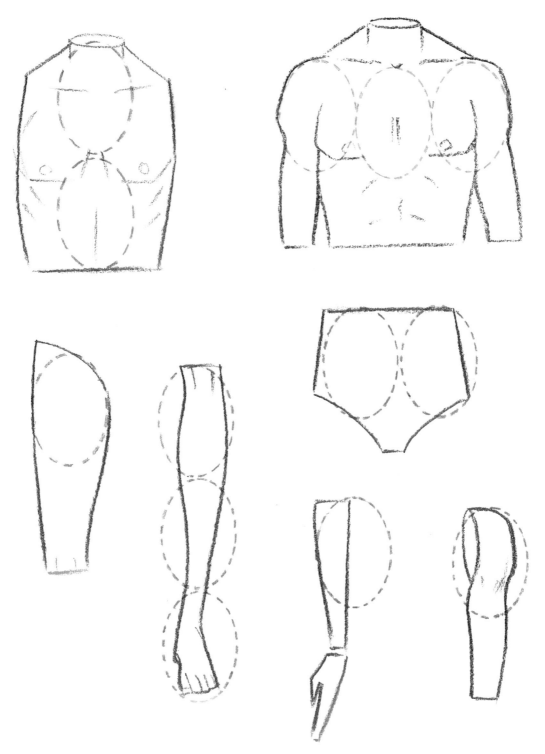

Figure 2.6 Upper torso/Shoulders/Shoulder and arm/
Lower torso/Hips to knees/Lower leg from knee to foot.

gender-neutral models have also been included in fashion media. Nevertheless, you must first master the canon before you can redefine it. Learn the basics of fashion proportion, and later, depending upon your own tastes, or the needs of your client, you may discard the standard fashion proportion for a proportion that better reflects you and your work.

In classical drawing, the common unit of measurement was—and remains—the head: It marks the various landmarks of the body and reveals the height and width of sections of the figure. As an example, where a man of average height might be about seven-and-a-half heads, the traditional male fashion figure would be nine heads.

While the choice of a fashion proportion varies according to the designer or illustrator, in the beginning it is best to adhere to the more common proportion of nine heads. Later, as you become more assured in your skills, you can settle on a stylized proportion that best suits your vision.

Each figure we create will be nine heads high. The height of the head, from the top of the skull to the chin, will be the rule for all vertical measurement, and the width of the head will be used for horizontal measurement (e.g., the shoulders or lower torso). Using this method, we can map out the body and make it easier to see the entire standing figure. To begin, the upper torso is the largest part of the body and is roughly two heads high.

The nine-head male shoulders are about three heads wide.

The upper arm and shoulder are a little shorter than the lower arm, including the hand: The shoulder itself is three-quarters of a head wide, and the rest of the arm and hand are about half a head wide.

The lower torso, from the hip bone to the groin, is slightly under two heads wide.

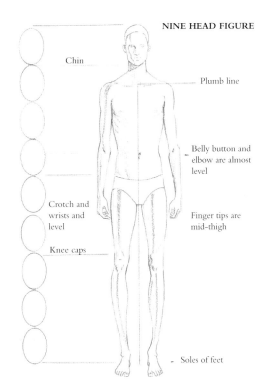

Figure 2.7 Figure with nine heads.

From the hips to the knees is two heads high and the thigh is one head wide.

The lower leg is slightly longer, at three heads long from knee to foot, and is a little more than half a head wide.

One way to gauge the correct proportions of a figure is to identify certain landmarks: The elbow is level with the navel, or mid-section, of the body; the wrist is parallel to the groin; and the hand is about two-thirds the length of a head.

Another guide is to split the figure in half: From the top of the head to the hip is four heads, and from the hip to the bottom of the foot is another four heads; add another head from the calf to the foot—thus stretching the height of the figure—and you have nine heads.

We are strictly concerned with the male fashion figure here; still, it is helpful to bear in

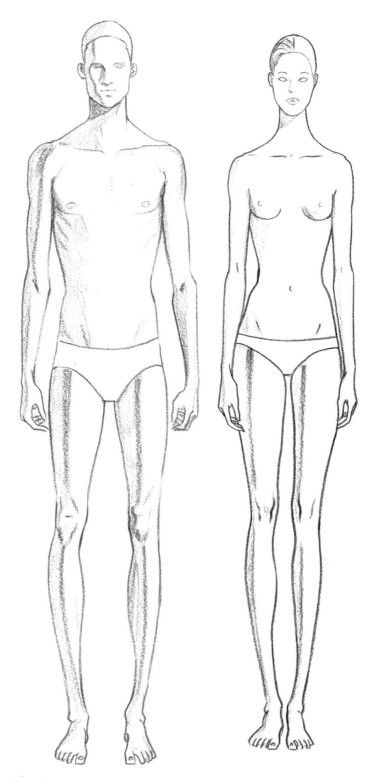

Figure 2.8 Male and female proportions.

mind the structural differences between the male and female figures. While both figures would conform to the nine-head formula, the female figure would be drawn slightly shorter than the male because of the measurements based on her smaller head.

The bones of the male are bigger and longer; the shoulders of a man are broader, but the pelvis or "hip section" is narrower than that of the female; men's arms are longer in proportion to the trunk than the female's; male legs are also longer (proportions may vary, depending on the figure you wish to illustrate). A plus-sized man might be wider, and, at seven heads, shorter, than a runway figure, which is very narrow, and shorter still next to a highly stylized figure of ten heads. Regardless of the figure's scale, its body parts, muscles and bones, still retain the same relative proportions.

Part of the process of learning to draw is training your eye to recognize the correct proportions. Using the head as a unit of measurement is helpful in the beginning, but you cannot draw all your figures with rulers and triangles. You must train your eyes to gauge proportions unaided— and that only comes with constant practice.

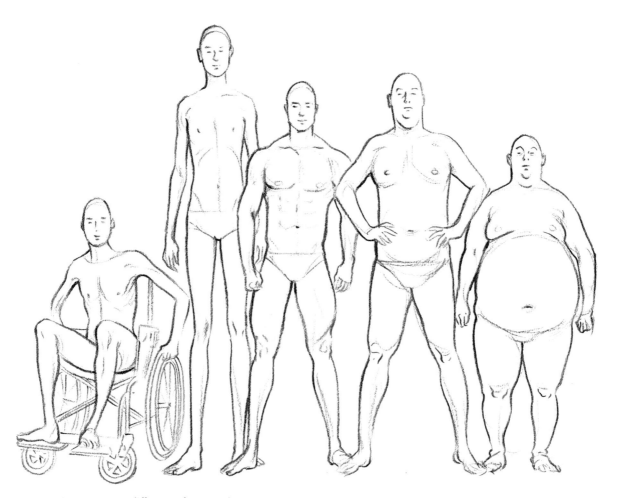

Figure 2.9 Five different male proportions.

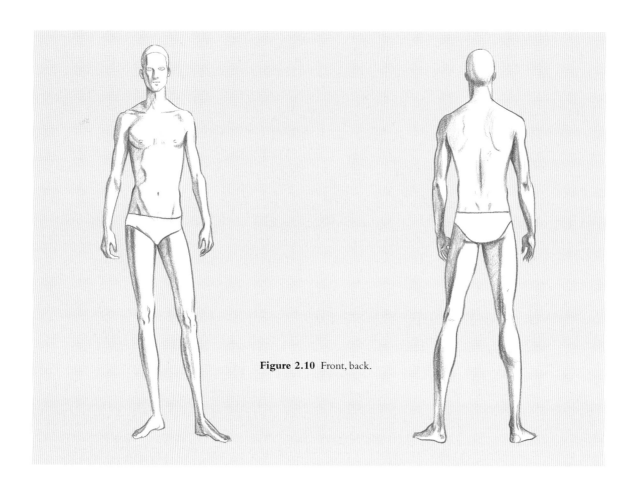

Figure 2.10 Front, back.

Basic Anatomy and the Simplified Construction of the Figure

Simply put, one cannot create a fashion design sketch, or an illustration, without rudimentary knowledge of the human body. Ignoring basic anatomy in a fashion drawing is like building a car without a chassis: Without an internal structure to bear the load of the outer shell, the car would collapse into a pile of unrecognizable parts. To extend the metaphor, the human figure is the vehicle of expression we have chosen to capture the look and feel of a garment in a drawing, so

understanding the skeletal structure of the body is key to a good fashion illustration.

In this chapter, we will study the essentials of figure construction and anatomy. Our focus will be on the relationship between muscle and bone, and how they work together. It is important that you take the time to carefully study the body's structure, but you aren't expected to memorize the names of all those bones and muscles—some of the names will stick, others will not—what matters is that you remember their functions, and their connections to each other. Equally vital is recognizing which bones, or muscles, affect the appearance of the clothed figure. In a fashion

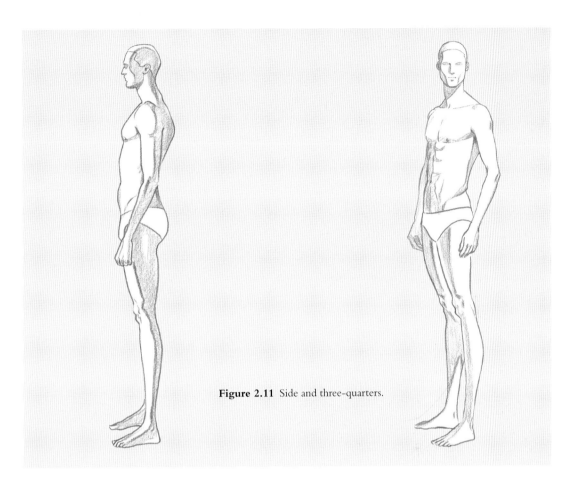

Figure 2.11 Side and three-quarters.

sketch, one should be able to sense the body beneath the clothes. As your knowledge of anatomy improves, you will be better able to sketch from memory.

THE PRINCIPAL BONES OF THE BODY

- **The skull** is a hard, egg-shaped bone structure, resting on the upper end of the spinal column.
- **The spinal column** is the center structure, or backbone, supporting the body; it comprises a series of small bones placed one atop the other, called vertebrae. The flexibility of this string of bones allows

the spine to bend, twist, turn, or remain erect. The spine also serves to protect the organs of the body.

- **The rib cage:** Below the clavicle, or collarbone, is a framework of bones called the rib cage. The ribs come around from each side of the spine and meet in front, along a flat bone called the sternum or breastbone.
- **The shoulder and arm bones:** The shoulders are suspended from the upper part of the rib cage in a shape known as the shoulder girdle. This connects the two upper arms to the structure of the rib cage, the clavicle, and the shoulder blades (or scapula). The larger arm bone, at the

top, is called the humerus. The lower part of the arm consists of two bones of equal size: The bone on the inside is known as the ulna, and the outside bone is known as the radius.

- **The thigh and leg bones:** The thigh bones, also known as femurs, are separated by the pelvis; these bones tilt inward, side by side, where they touch. The lower leg contains two bones. The larger is called the tibia, or shinbone; located on the outside, and slightly behind, is the smaller bone, known as the fibula. The proper name for the bone that is commonly called the kneecap is "patella."

- **The bones of the foot:** The lower ends of the two leg bones, the tibia and the fibula, join to form the ankle joints. The inside ankle joint is slightly higher than the outside ankle joint; the foot is arched. The foot bones are bound by ligaments, giving the foot movement and solidity.

THE MUSCLES OF THE BODY

If the bones represent the framework and structure of the body, then the muscles serve as the covering that affects the surface of the body. Muscles are the soft tissue that not only gives shape and form to the physique, but also functions to produce force and movement. While women have the same muscles as men, their muscles are generally smaller and less pronounced. The musculature of the male fashion figure is not to be confused with that of a comic book superhero, but neither should it look like the average man on the street. In addition to being taller, the typical male fashion figure is thinner. His chest and shoulders are broad, but the legs and arms, though muscular, are longer and slimmer.

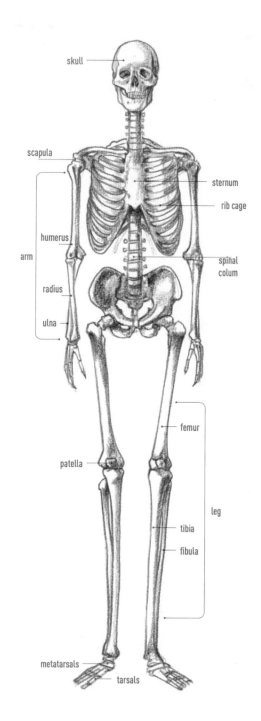

Figure 2.12a Skeleton.

While it is useful to learn the various names of muscles, remembering their function and appearance is more important to an artist. There are many more muscles than bones, so we will simplify this phase of anatomy by referring to only those major muscle groups that have the most to do with the outward look of the body.

- **The pectoralis major** is a large, fan-shaped muscle in the pectoral region that is responsible for the movement of the shoulder joint.
- **The deltoid** is a round, tapered muscle located at the top of the shoulder and the upper side of the arm.
- **The rectus abdominis**, also known as "abs," is a paired muscle group lying vertically on each side of the abdomen. The two muscles are separated by a band of connective tissue called the *linea alba*.
- **The biceps** is the larger muscle in the upper arm that flexes the arm and forearm.
- **The triceps** is a large muscle on the back of the upper arm. It is responsible for the extension of the elbow joint which straightens the arm.
- **The rectus femoris**, commonly known as the quadriceps, is the muscle attached to the hip, and helps to raise and extend the knee.
- **The gastrocnemius** is the large muscle of the calf. Running to the Achilles tendon from two heads attached to the femur, it enables the flexing of the knee and foot.
- **The brachioradialis** is the muscle of the forearm that flexes the forearm at the elbow.
- **The semitendinosus** is one of three hamstring muscles located at the back of the thigh.

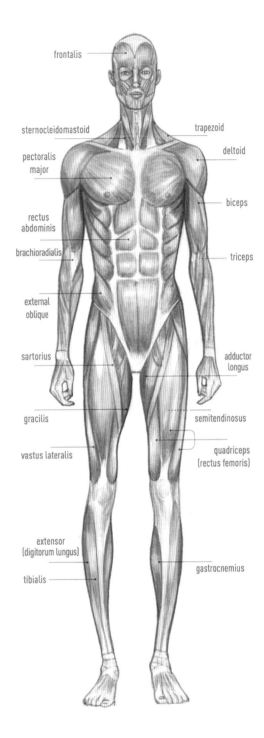

Figure 2.12b Muscles.

A Simplified Construction of the Figure

As stated earlier, a thorough knowledge of human anatomy is key to drawing a convincing figure, but when one adds the other thousand-and-one biological details facing the artist, figuring out where to start, and how, can be intimidating, so it's best to begin by whittling the figure down to an easy-to-understand size. One way to look at the figure is to reduce it to a series of simple basic forms. The head becomes an egg shape; the neck is a short column; the upper torso is a three-dimensional barrel connected to a line representing the spine; that line is connected to the lower torso, a slightly smaller barrel; upper and lower arms, and upper and lower legs, are represented by modified cylinders, and the joints become small spheres. The hands and feet are now cubed, and coned, forms. By reducing the figure to these simple solid forms, you will begin to understand not only the separate essential parts of the body, but also their relationships to one another, and their three-dimensional form.

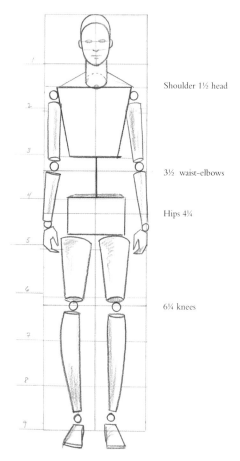

Shoulder 1½ head

3½ waist-elbows

Hips 4¼

6¼ knees

Figure 2.13 Block form of figure.

The Upper Torso

Students often view the upper and lower torso as an undifferentiated block of muscle and bone. This is not true, but it does help to explain why many figure drawings look stiff. Think of the torso as consisting of three masses: the chest, the abdomen, and the pelvis. The chest, or rib cage, is shaped like a three-sided cage, and because the ribs and pelvis are made of bone, they are fairly rigid. The abdominal mass, which contains no bone, is flexible, and is why the waist is flexible. The clavicle, the rib cage, the sternum, and the shoulder blades are supported by the spine, and cover and protect the internal organs.

The front of the torso has a furrow traversing the full length of the torso. Beginning at the pit of the neck, it runs through the chest, dividing the pectoral muscles, continues through the navel, and ends at the pubic bone. A similar furrow marks the center of the back; this organic dividing line serves to remind us of the symmetry of the human body. Abstracting the torso into two barrels or cubes—thereby abstracting the upper and lower torso—separated and attached by a line representing the spine, and then adding muscles, will help give your figures dimensionality and flexibility.

Arms, Legs, Hands, and Feet

THE ARM AND HAND

Although we have already discussed the basic anatomy of the arm, and the combination of bones and muscles that make up the structure, a brief review of the arm and a closer look at the hand is in order. As stated previously, the front view of the arm will show the deltoid, biceps, and forearm. The back and side view will include the triceps. From the armpit, where the arm separates from the body, the arm will gradually taper to the elbow, becoming larger after the elbow and then becoming smaller at the wrist. The hand joins at the wrist.

THE HAND

The hand is viewed by many artists as one of the more difficult parts of the human anatomy to draw, and it is easy to understand why. The hand is a complicated structure: It is easy to understand and yet confusing to render. Therefore, it may be helpful to think of the hand as having two masses: The first, the palm, is a square mass; the second, the thumb, is an adjoining mass. The thumb is at a right angle to the hand and moves independently of the other fingers. The other

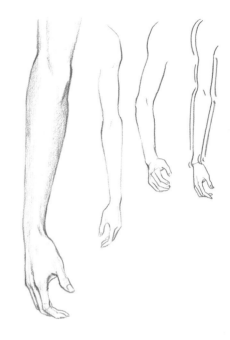

Figure 2.14 Arm and hand.

four fingers vary in size, with the middle finger being the longest. There are three bones in each finger, starting with the knuckle. The knuckles of the hand form an arc which is repeated in the middle and end joints of the fingers.

The bones of the hand fan out from the wrist. When the hand is open, the fingers form an apex. Viewed from the side, the fingers are like three steps that taper down to the fingertips. In comparison to the female hand, the male hand is wider and somewhat squarer. If we continue to use the head as a unit of measure, the hand would be the length of the face from chin to mid-forehead. The easiest way to draw the hand is to abstract it into a series of basic forms, either

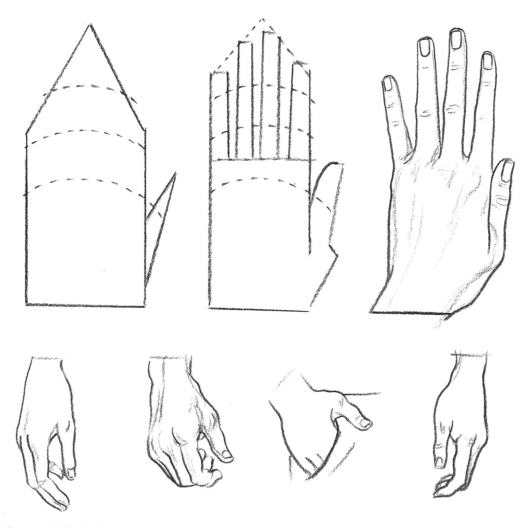

Figure 2.15 The hand.

breaking the structure into block forms or creating a simple silhouette.

Observation and simplification are key in learning how to draw hands. Unlike other parts of the body, the subtle changes in how the hand looks and operates requires careful study. Try sketching hands at every opportunity. As mentioned earlier, only by drawing, and learning from the inevitable mistakes in your drawing, will you improve. The more you sketch, the more you'll learn.

THE LEG AND THE FOOT

The leg is made up of three basic parts: the thigh, the lower leg, and the foot. The thigh is wide near the pelvis and then narrows toward the

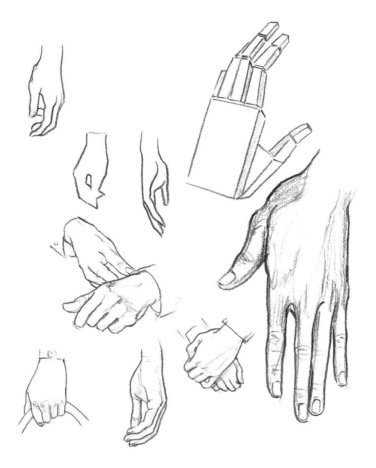

Figure 2.16 Hands.

knee. It is made up of three sets of muscles the hamstring muscles in the back of the thigh, the quadriceps muscles in the front, and the adductor muscles on the inside. Like the arm, the leg tapers from top to bottom.

The heaviness of the thigh is due to the thick muscles, which must not only provide locomotion, but also carry the weight of the body. The knee is a hinged joint that allows for backward and forward motion. From there the leg widens a bit to shape the calf and then tapers gradually to the ankle and foot. The calf muscle, the gastrocnemius, is a large muscle; it has two parts, or "heads," which create the diamond shape. The soleus is a smaller, flat muscle underneath the gastrocnemius muscle. Both the gastrocnemius and the soleus muscles taper and merge at the base of the calf muscle. When drawing the leg, note the curves of the leg from the front and back, as well as the profile. The silhouetted lines of the leg are never parallel.

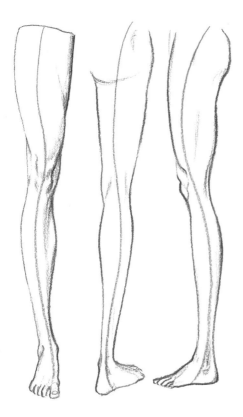

Figure 2.17 The leg and foot.

front, the ankles appear curved, with the inner ankle bone higher than the outer.

While all the five toes support the weight of the body, the big toe is made to carry the heaviest load. The direction of the foot will determine the order in which you see the toes. Viewed from the outside, the small, or baby, toe will be seen first, with the other toes following. From the inside or interior side view, the big toe will be seen first, with the other toes following in order.

In summary, the fashion figure, as described here, is based on both the elongated proportions of fashion art and the classical proportions of Western fine art. Knowing such proportions are essential for every fashion artist. This does not mean that an artist, or designer, cannot vary their own proportions; the freedom to decide how to paint or draw a figure is up to the individual. Ideally, however, an artist should create from knowledge rather than guessing; to put it another way, it is easier to stretch or break the rules once you know what they are.

The connective tissue at the bottom of the calf merges into the Achilles tendon. The tibia, or shinbone, is the prominent bone in the middle of the lower leg.

Drawing the Male Head

It's not always necessary—or even desirable—for a fashion sketch to be a detailed portrait, but you must know the proper placement of features on a head. Few things reveal character, or individuality, like a face. In most figurative art the head is the focal point, and this is particularly true in fashion illustration. Just as a person's face might clue us into who they are, the head of a good fashion figure can show us who, ideally, would wear such a garment. Moreover, an interesting, or compelling, face can establish a connection between the artist and the viewer.

THE FOOT

The foot is essentially a platform that supports the weight of the body, and the easiest way to view the foot is as a wedge. The top side is flat and forms a slope. The outer side is a long triangle that is flat on the ground, and the inner side has an arch that creates a bridge between the ball of the foot and the heel. The ankle joins the leg and foot together. The heel bone at the back juts out and forms a separate wedge. Viewed from the

Just as there are landmarks that help us remember the placement of sections of the body,

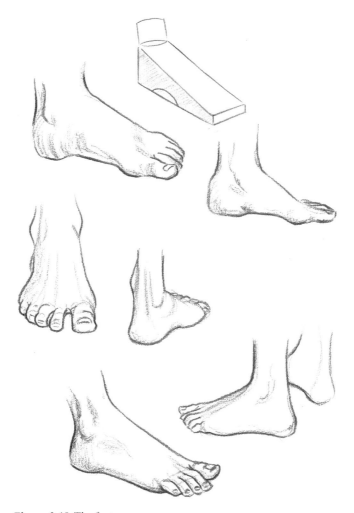

Figure 2.18 The foot.

there are ways of observing the proportions of the head through certain guidelines; keep in mind that while faces vary according to age, weight, and ethnicity, the placement of the eyes, nose, ears, and mouth are, with some exceptions, universal. Many fashion artists stylize their heads, creating faces that reflect their own ideas of contemporary beauty. Study these different versions of fashion heads and learn from them. Once you have mastered the fundamentals, you can explore different ways to stylize the head.

What follows are the basic proportions for the adult male head.

BLOCKING IN THE HEAD: THE FRONT VIEW

1. First, draw an egg-shaped sphere, with the round part at the top and the narrow end at the bottom. Make sure the oval is not too thin or too circular. Add a truncated column for the neck (only slightly narrower

Figure 2.19 Top right: Velicia Gourdin; Bottom right: George Gozum; Bottom middle: Eddie Redmayne by Carlos Aponte; Middle left: Richard Vyse; Top left: Ejpt by Clifford Faust. Second and third on the right, middle box second row from the bottom and bottom box on the left are by the author.

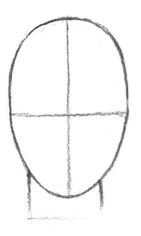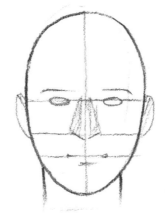

Figure 2.20 Blocking in the head: front view.

than the width of the oval). Draw horizontal and vertical center lines; these will act as guidelines.

2. Draw another horizontal line to divide the lower part of the face. Then draw another line dividing that space.

3. **The mouth** is formed on the last horizontal line. To determine the width of the mouth, drop a line down from the inside of each pupil. The upper lip is somewhat thinner, while the lower lip is fuller and rounder.

4. **The jawline** is somewhat square, with the lip line indicating the beginning of the jaw. Men typically have a heavier jawline than women, and many illustrators exaggerate that feature.

BLOCKING IN THE HEAD: THE PROFILE

1. Draw an egg-shaped oval in profile. Divide the head in half with a horizontal line,

divide the space in half, then divide it in half again.

2. Draw the brow, nose, lips, and chin in profile—remember that the eyes, nose, and ear are in alignment. Indicate the hairline.

3. Add details and indicate shadows, if any, under the nose and chin.

BLOCKING IN THE HEAD: THREE-QUARTER VIEW

1. Draw an egg-shaped oval in a three-quarter view. Draw a curved vertical center line, with the side closest to you making up at least two-thirds of the head.

2. Divide the face in half horizontally, and divide that space in half again; the next line, which will provide the guideline for the mouth, lands on the upper third of the remaining bottom.

3. Refine the head by adding first the nose, then the eyes, paying careful attention to the foreshortened eye and lips.

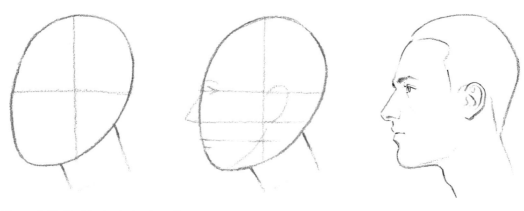

Figure 2.21 Blocking in the head: profile.

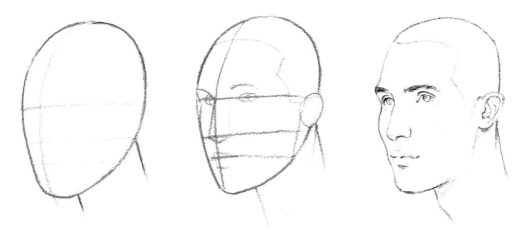

Figure 2.22 Blocking in the head: three-quarter view.

TILTING THE HEAD FORWARD AND BACKWARD

Draw an egg-shaped oval representing the head. When the head is viewed from below or above eye level, the measuring lines become more curved in shape. The spaces are no longer equal. Here, strict observation of the model is necessary. A head looking down will show a larger portion of the forehead. The eyes and ears line up and become more prominent, and the chin will recede and become smaller.

A head that tilts up will force the nose and the jawline into more prominence. The ears will be lower in relation to the eyes, with the lips and brow becoming more pronounced.

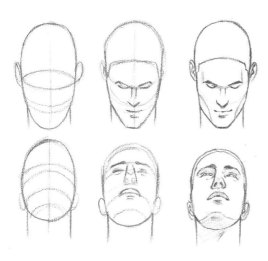

Figure 2.23 Blocking in the head: tilting the head forward and backward.

THE FEATURES

The eyes

From the front, the easiest way to envision the eye is as an oval, with a heavy dark line slightly above it registering as the eyebrow. The eye is in a socket. This eye socket is a bony cup within the forehead. The eyebrows border the socket and extend over it. These features protect the eyes. The upper lid of the eye opens and closes over the curved eyeball, while the lower lid rarely moves. The eyeball is oval and consists of the pupil, iris, and cornea, and the sclera, or white of the eye. When drawing the eye from the front, start with an oval. The upper lid should be drawn as a slight fold. It should also mask a part of the pupil, so that the eye doesn't appear to be registering shock. The corners of the eye should narrow. Symmetry is important here; an uneven eye or eyebrow can seem amateurish or just off. Remember that the upper and lower lids are lined with eyelashes, which read as dark lines, heavier on the upper lid than the lower. The pupils are round but partially covered by the upper lid.

In a three-quarter view, the shape of the eye becomes a long and exaggerated egg-shaped oval. Though both eyes are similar in appearance, the nearer eye is longer than the farther one. The profile eye is a simple v-shape, creating both the upper and lower lid. The pupil becomes a convex or rounded curve shape fitted in the v-shape.

A profile view of the eye is perhaps the easiest to draw. The eye, foreshortened, becomes a horizontal v-shape with a narrow convex pupil. When the eye is open, the lid is folded under. When the eye is closed, the lid is smooth.

The eyebrows on a man are generally heavier and less curved than a woman's brow.

The nose

One way to remember the structure of a nose is to think of it as a slim wedge with two sides and a top. It protrudes from the face, causing shadows under the nostrils, or shadows from one side or another, depending on the direction of the light. The upper, bony part starts at the bridge, a triangle-shaped flat surface between the eyebrows, and continues to mid-eye level. It then narrows, ending about halfway down the length of the nose. The rest is made of cartilage. As the nose narrows, it becomes rounder at the end, becoming a bulb. The bulb, or tip, separates into two nostrils enclosed by wings. The nostrils are seen as two dark hollows. Most illustrators typically draw one side, merely hinting at the nostrils. Whatever the abbreviated or abstracted version of the nose, its relation to both the eyes and mouth is very important. Obviously, there are as many different types of noses as there are people, so observation is key. Your rendering of the nose will depend on how realistic, or stylized and abstract, your approach is.

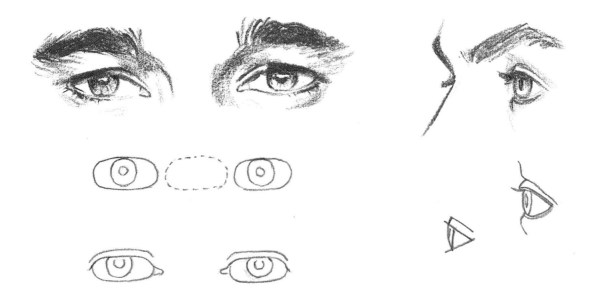

The Eyes

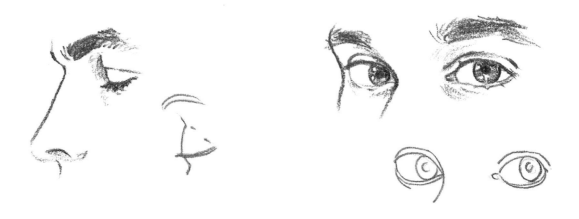

Figure 2.24 The eyes.

The Nose

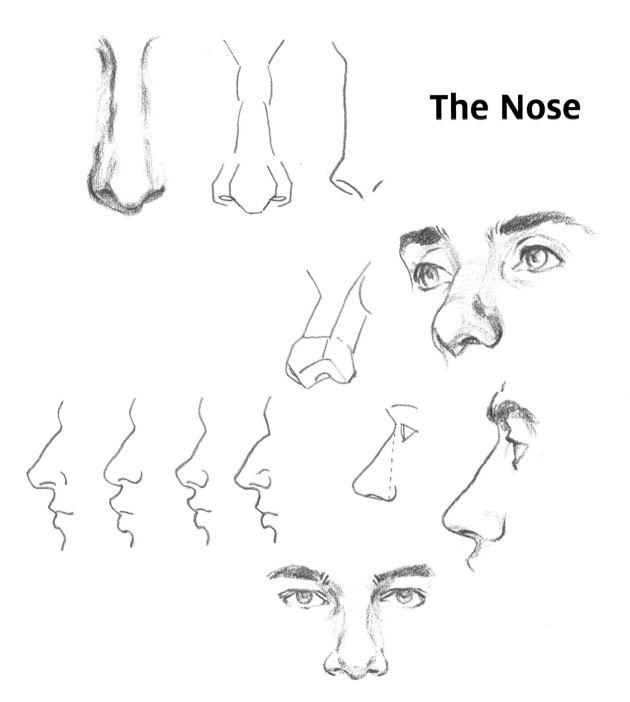

Figure 2.25 The nose.

The Mouth

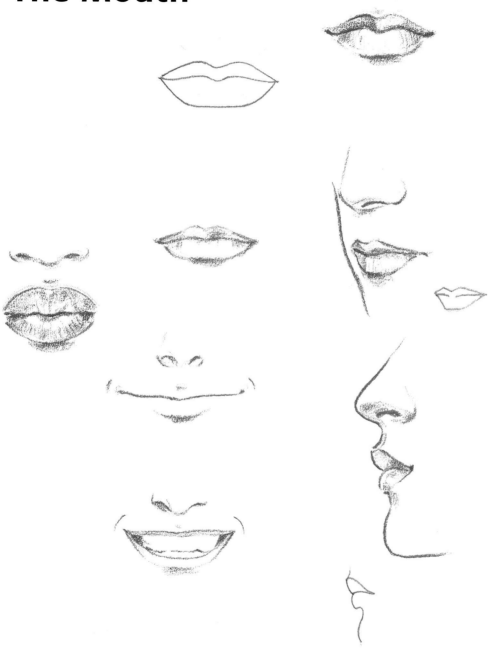

Figure 2.26 The mouth.

The mouth

Other than the eyes, the mouth is probably the most expressive feature of the face. Pursed lips can indicate annoyance or pique, while a down-turned mouth might suggest sadness or disapproval. The faces of many fashion figures are limited to one of two expressions: blank handsomeness or cheery self-satisfaction. There is nothing wrong with that, but a face with some character can add to the uniqueness of your drawing. Careful study and experimentation of faces can lend your heads a distinctive look, showcasing your individuality as an artist.

The shape of the mouth is determined by the shape of the teeth. The upper lip is divided into three parts; the lower lip has two. Most upper lips project slightly over the lower lip because of the natural overbite of the teeth; this is most noticeable in profile. The shape of the mouth varies according to age, gender, and ethnicity. Some mouths have lips that are fuller, some thinner. Start with a thinner upper lip and suggest a wider and fuller bottom lip as a starting point. Pay particular attention to the outer ends of the lips; these can help indicate a range of expressions. For example, when smiling, both corners of the mouth are pulled back, with the lips pressed against the teeth, lightly elongating the lips. Generally speaking, the male fashion mouth is less defined than its female counterpart. A close-up of a male fashion face would require more attention to detail than a full figure sketch, where the emphasis would be on the garment. Most male fashion figures only suggest the mouth with a few deft lines. However, practice is key: Drawing mouths, either from life or from photographs, is always a good idea.

Drawing hair

As with a live model, a fashion figure's looks can be enhanced by an appropriate hairstyle. A fashion drawing is meant to translate the aesthetic viewpoint of the designer or the customer, so any details that add to that are a plus. Think about how the hair looks with the clothing, both as a graphic element and as an accessory to the clothes being drawn. Long hair might obstruct or hide a garment detail around the neck and shoulder; a large afro might interfere with the hood on a sweatshirt. Always consider those choices that would best communicate and enhance the style of the garment.

To begin, remember that the hairline starts approximately one-third from the top of the head. Typically, there is less hair on the sides of the head. Start by drawing the overall shape of the hair. Then create a few lines that indicate the direction and texture of the hair: straight, curly, or kinky? These lines, thick and thin, should follow the natural outgrowth and movement of the hair from the hairline to the areas near the ears and neck—too many lines look amateurish, so limit your lines in the beginning. Keep in mind that the hair should be in proportion to the head you have created. Facial hair—beards, mustaches, goatees, etc.—are on the lower half of the face but follow the same approach: Draw the shape of the hair, and then draw a few lines to show the direction of growth. Next, add shadows and highlights. Think of your light source. If the light is above, then there will be highlights on the crown of the head, and possibly the forehead if there are bangs or a pompadour.

Many artists find drawing men's heads liberating: Whereas women's fashion heads are often dictated by ever-changing seasonal ideas of beauty, and thus highly stylized, men's fashion heads don't change as rapidly. Study fashion magazines and other media for inspiration. Remember to think of the head as a three-dimensional object,

Figure 2.27 Drawing hair.

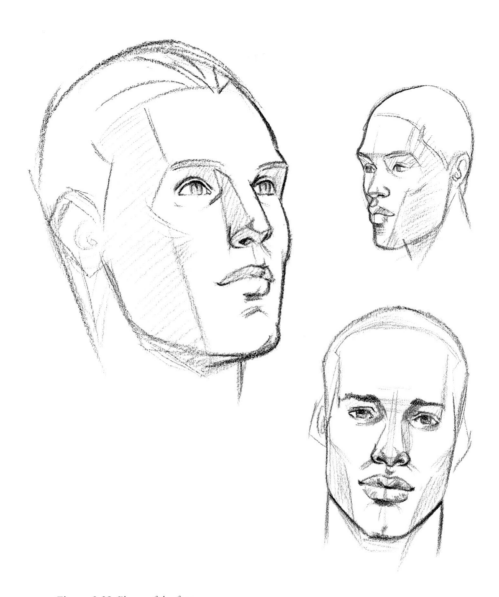

Figure 2.28 Planes of the face.

and not a flat mask. It might be helpful to view the head as existing in a cube with six sides. There is the top of the head, the front, or face, the back and sides, and then the underside of the jaw. Drawing the head with an awareness of projecting planes like those of the forehead, nose, cheekbones, and chin, along with light and shaded areas, will help give your head the depth

and authority you want. Character lines and facial hair can also aid in defining a man's face and character.

Experiment by drawing different heads with different features and haircuts. Explore different versions of contemporary male beauty as they relate to ethnicity and age—and don't be limited by realism.

Art Supplies: The Tools of an Artist

Art supplies are the tools that allow the artist to express what they are trying to say. And, as in any profession, the right tools are paramount. Once an artist learns how to use their media, they can then expand the media to fit their vision. One must learn the rules before one can break them. By experimenting with different mediums, you will discover which ones naturally appeal to you, and which ones don't.

In Chapters 1 through 3 you will need only pencils, erasers, newsprint paper or all-purpose paper, and tracing paper.

First, consider your work area. You will need a comfortable surface to draw and paint on. Most illustrators and designers use a drafting, or drawing, table (easels are used mainly for life drawing).

- **A drafting table** is a multipurpose desk with a surface that tilts. The best ones are adjustable and should be able to tilt to an angle preferred by the artist. Any comfortable chair will do, but there are chairs made especially for drafting tables. These chairs can change height, lean backward or forward, and, if they have wheels, they can move. Your choice of seating will be determined by the angle of your drawing table, and what you are willing to spend.
- **Lighting comes next:** Be sure to work in a well-lit area and equip your workspace with the proper lighting. Popular among many artists are combination art lamps. These lamps emit a full spectrum of light: a combination of warm light (think

Figure 2.29 Art supplies.

incandescent) and cool light (fluorescent) that color-corrects your work. LED lights are also popular. As a designer, or illustrator, color will be an important part of your work: Proper lighting ensures that the color you create will be the actual color as printed or presented.

- **Pencils**, commonly called "lead" pencils, are made of graphite. They come in gradations that range from H, for hard—usually used in technical drawings—to B, for the blackness of the mark. The gradations range from 9H—very hard; the pencil mark is very light—to 9B, which makes the softest, and darkest, marks. HB, hard and black, lands in the middle of the scale.

- **Graphite sticks** lack the wood casing of regular pencils. A versatile drawing medium, and a favorite with art students and professionals, graphite comes in various degrees of hardness. The harder the stick, the lighter the stroke, while the softer sticks exhibit a smooth darker stroke. Graphite sticks come in flat sticks and pencils.

- **Pastels** are an old painting medium, and although they are like chalk, they are not the same. Chalk is made of limestone or gypsum compressed into sticks. Soft pastels are made from mineral pigments, like those used in watercolor, oil paints, or acrylics, and is combined with gum tragacanth and water. Pressed into square or rounded sticks, pastels create a soft powdery mark that is suitable for covering large areas or producing sharp lines. Oil pastels are made from a non-drying oil and a wax bonder. They leave a thick

waxy mark with a denser, more intense hue. When combined with turpentine, they create an interesting buttery smudge that is neither pastel nor paint. All pastels require a paper with a texture, or tooth, that allows the pastel to adhere to its surface.

- **Color pencils** are easy to use and carry around, making them a perfect medium for use outdoors. Within the context of fashion drawing, they are often used alone, or in conjunction with markers. Colored pencils have a core made of colored pigment, chalk, wax, and additives and binding agents. They come in hard and soft varieties, they work well on their own or with watercolor and markers, and they are great for adding shadows or details to a figure. Color pencils are like graphite pencils but less messy. They come in sets ranging from 12 to 120 or can be bought individually.

- **Watercolor pencils** are water-soluble colored pencils made with coloring pigments that stain when they come in contact with water. Drawing with watercolor pencils is like drawing with regular colored pencils—just add wet brushstrokes to dissolve the pigments.

- **China markers**, also known as grease pencils or *Chinagraphs*, are wax pencils that were originally developed for use on photographic contact sheets and other glossy surfaces like glass or plastic; the marks they make are bolder and heavier than regular pencils. China markers are versatile and work well on newsprint and all-purpose paper. They are available in many colors, including black. The down-side is that a China marker line cannot be erased.

- **Charcoal**, perhaps the oldest medium, is another alternative. The difference between charcoal and graphite is one of density. Charcoal is dry and somewhat brittle, while graphite is oily and slick. Natural charcoal sticks have a tonal range from light gray to jet black, depending on the pressure of the strokes and the density of the charcoal. It is the easiest medium for creating tones and shading. Wood-encased charcoal is generally cheaper and less messy.

- **A pencil sharpener** is strongly suggested, preferably an electric or battery-operated one, though at a pinch a small hand sharpener will do.

- **Erasers** are a good idea. No one is perfect, and erasers make life easier by allowing us to continue a drawing when we're tempted to throw it away because of a mistake. There are pink, white, and gum erasers for general use, but kneaded erasers are especially prized. They don't leave eraser residue, crumbs, or the occasional smear, and can remove pencil lines without tearing the paper. They're also good for creating highlights in heavily penciled drawings.

- **A marker** is a type of pen used to create permanent or semi-permanent marks on paper. Invented in 1952, markers today come in a bewildering assortment of colors. They are affordable and easy to use and have become a popular media for beginner and professional alike. They can be purchased individually or in sets, and come with different nibs—fine, medium, broad, and chiseled; many markers have at least two nibs. It is often best to buy color markers separately, and slowly build a personal collection that reflects your own palette, rather than buying a set of markers with colors you will never use. It is also best to try out markers before purchasing.

- **Drawing pens**, also known as technical pens or drafting pens, are art tools typically used by architects, engineers, and illustrators. These pens have needle-point tips in an assortment of widths from 0.15 mm to 0.50 mm, making them perfect for detailed line work and fashion figure outlines. Some examples on the market are: Rapidograph Technical pens, Sakura Pigma Micron pens, Pilot Drawing pens, Faber-Castell Pitt drawing pens, and the Staedtler Pigment Liner. Another version of the drawing pen is the gel pen. A particular favorite is the white gel pen. These pens have a thick, opaque ink, much like paint, and are best used for rendering fine details, texture, or embellishments against a dark color background.

- **Watercolors** are water-soluble pigments in tube or cake form; both types can be purchased individually or in sets. For a beginner, Sennelier French Artists' Watercolor set and Cotman are a good place to start. The next step up would be Winsor & Newton or M. Graham & Co. Most artists prefer buying individual tube paint. Prices vary according to brand and quality. Starting out, you might want to buy an inexpensive set to experiment with. Later, you may decide to purchase colors separately and build your own set of colors. When working with water-color tubes, you will need a palette (see below) or mixing dish, a water jar, and (clean) rags or paper towels. Cake sets often have built-in paint wells. Gouache paints, also sold in tube and cake form, are an opaque form of watercolor. The opacity of gouache is due to the chalk or white pigment that is added to the color pigment and binding, making it less transparent. They resemble the poster or finger paints used by young children.

- **Drawing inks:** Though not as popular as they once were, drawing inks can be an alternative to watercolor. Fast-drying, water-soluble—but water-resistant—and transparent, drawing inks are easy to use. Some inks are opaque and waterproof; these can be difficult to work with, so choose carefully. Translucent drawing inks can be used with a brush, a pen, or an airbrush, and their colors often have a richness and vibrancy that watercolor does not always have. Many inks are water-based with shellac as an additive, so make sure you rinse your brush and pen thoroughly after use.

- **Paper** comes in different sizes and weights. American and European drawing paper sizes are different. **A4** paper is an International/European paper size established by the the International Standards Organization (ISO); it measures 210 × 297 mm or 8.27 × 11.69 inches. **A3** measures 297 × 420 mm or 11 × 17 inches. **A2** measures 420 × 594 mm or 17 × 22 inches, and **A1** measures 594 ×

841 mm or 22 × 34 inches. Your choice will depend upon the intended use. **All-purpose paper** is a good option for a variety of media, works well with pencil and marker, and is usually inexpensive. **Newsprint** is an off-white paper that is usually used for life drawing and sketching rather than finished illustrations. It, too, is very inexpensive. **Tracing paper**, a thin translucent paper, is often used to redraw or correct work in progress; like many of the papers mentioned, it comes in pads of various sizes. **Vellum** is a heavy, transparent paper that works well with a variety of media. **Textured paper** is self-explanatory. It includes corrugated boards, embossed papers, mesh, and woven and hand-crafted papers. **Tinted paper** is often used with pastel art but can also be used for artwork that requires an extreme contrast of values, like white paint on gray paper.

- **Graphite paper**, also known as transfer paper, is used to transfer a drawing onto another drawing surface. It is similar to carbon paper, but much cleaner. To use, tape your drawing paper onto a firm, flat surface, then place a sheet of tracing paper with your rough drawing on top of it. Tape it so the rough drawing does not move. Place the graphite paper— graphite side down—between the tracing paper and the clean drawing paper, then, applying some pressure, trace your rough image onto the drawing paper. **Marker paper** is made especially for marker use, and is usually slightly see-through. **Illustration board** is drawing paper mounted on both sides of a heavy board, creating a stiff surface. These boards come in varying thicknesses and work well with different media; they come in different colors and are also good for mounting artwork.

- **Watercolor paper** is sold in different finishes (or surfaces). A *hot press* surface has a smooth, satiny finish which allows the paint to dry quickly. *Cold press* has a slightly textured finish, in-between a hot press and a rough surface, which has a more prominent tooth, or textured surface. Rough paper will hold the water-color on its surface, taking a longer time to dry. The thickness of watercolor paper is determined by its weight: 90 lb. (190 gsm), 140 lb. (300 gsm), 260 lb. (356 gsm), and 300 lb. (638 gsm). How you paint will determine the weight of your paper: 90 lb. watercolor paper might be too thin for a very wet approach. For the beginner, an assortment pack of different weights and textures might be ideal. For most designers and illustrators, 140 lb. paper should suffice. Watercolor paper is sold in single sheets, packs, pads, and blocks. As with all art supplies, prices will vary with quality; for the beginner, a less expensive paper will work fine.

- **Brushes:** The best watercolor brushes are sable. There are many synthetic brushes that can work just as well, but sable comes the most highly recommended. One might start with sizes #1, #3, #6, and #8. As you progress you may want a #10, or even some smaller sizes. Keep in mind that some brushes are made to create loose, flexible lines, while others are best for areas of wash. Unlike oil brushes, watercolor brushes are defined by their slightly rounded or pointed tips. They come in a variety of sizes, but numbers 6 through 9 are best for figure painting. Cheap brushes will lose their tapered points and become fuzzy and mop-like; this is less likely to happen with more expensive brands. Good brushes are an investment, so keep them in good condition. Build your brush collection slowly, experimenting with different sizes and effects. Gradually, over time, you will discover which brushes work best for you. *Always keep your brushes clean.* When finished with your brush, be sure to shake off the excess water and create a point, and let it dry, brush-side up or on its side.

- **Palettes:** A watercolor palette is a plate with several wells for holding and mixing colors. They come in many sizes and types. There are enameled palettes, plastic ones, and metal ones. A simple and inexpensive palette is a porcelain tray known as a butcher's tray. It's a good size, and because of its finish it is easy to clean. There are also individual cups or small bowls that can serve the same purpose. Again, these can be found in any art supply store. Make sure that the wells are fairly deep so that they can hold a good amount of color or tone wash. A damp paper towel over your paints will keep them moist.

- A **Lightbox** is an illuminated surface used by artists to trace rough pencil sketches on another drawing surface for the finished illustration. The device is also used to view photographic films. Lightboxes can be found in most art supply stores and come in a variety of sizes with corresponding prices.

REFERENCE FILES

A reference file, also known as a swipe file, is an important tool for illustrators and designers; it is a curated collection of images that you have organized as personal research. You can create files for things like poses, faces, coats, pants, and environments, or for inspiration: other illustrations or paintings, color combinations, fabric swatches, or art techniques. Think of your files as a ready source of information when you need to work on a certain pose or image. Swipes are valuable resources when you don't have a live model and you need an example of how a figure would look in a particular pose. A swipe file can be a collection of magazine or newspaper clippings in different folders, or a digital collection on your desktop, in your digital files, or on sites like Instagram or Pinterest.

Men's fashion magazines like *GQ*, *Esquire*, and *L'Uomo Vogue*, to name a few, can also be valuable resources. Not only must you familiarize yourself with the latest fashions, but such magazines can also be a resource for poses and specific fabrics.

3

Movement

Movement is a bit of a misnomer when discussing fashion design sketches. Since the aim of a design drawing is to accurately convey the look and proportion of a garment, any exaggerated movement—running, jumping, sitting, etc.—would distort the lines of the clothing, making a precise assessment of the garment difficult. So, for the purposes of this chapter, by "movement" I mean the myriad of subtle positions that give expression to the figure. In this chapter I will discuss how to create a figure that has a sense of energy even when the figure is merely standing.

The Balance or Center Line

While it may appear counter-intuitive, drawing a body that appears to be standing straight is the first step in creating a figure with a suggestion of movement. The key here is balance.

A balanced figure is one that seems to stand erect and doesn't look as though it is falling over. Balance is the subtle distribution of weight that enables human beings to stand. An aid to finding that balance in a figure is the center line, also called the plumb or "axial line." This configuration is an imaginary vertical line that begins at the pit of the neck and lands on the leg and foot that is supporting the weight of the body. When the figure is standing erect, the weight is evenly distributed on both sides of the body; when the weight shifts, the center line will transfer over to whichever leg is supporting the weight of the body. The shifting of weight from one leg to another will cause one leg to relax, with that side of the hip dropping down a bit, while the other leg will straighten, pushing up that side of the hip.

Figure 3.1 Image courtesy of Leonard Cadiente. @bycadiente lcadiente2006@mac.com.

Figure 3.2a Upper torso in profile.

Figure 3.2b The mechanics of construction and movement.

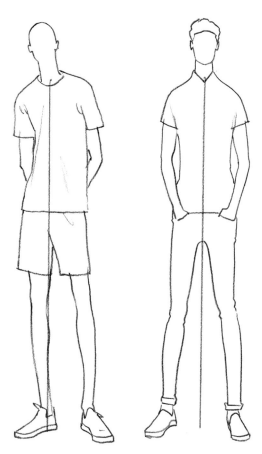

Figure 3.3a The plumb line.

When drawing the figure, begin by drawing a straight line to establish your center front. The line should be sketched lightly—remember, it is only a guide. As with all rules, there are exceptions: The movements of the arms may affect the distribution of weight around the center line, and movement from the upper torso may obscure your center line. Whether working from a photograph or a live model, note that the body is centered on a vertical line for balance, regardless of the direction of the model.

Figure 3.3b The plumb line.

Action Lines

Action lines illustrate the direction of the shoulders and hips. Because of the spine, the upper and lower torso can move independently of one another. Action lines above the waistline follow one direction, while below the waist the lines follow the opposite direction. The subtle twisting and turning of the torso can give a figure a sense of movement. When one side is stressed or active, the other side might be compressed. All of this is possible because of the spine: The angle of the shoulders and the hips, and the ability of the body to twist and bend, is due to its flexibility.

Think of the spine as a rod connecting not only the upper and lower parts of the torso, but the head and shoulders as well. Try to imagine the action lines whenever you look at a fashion figure.

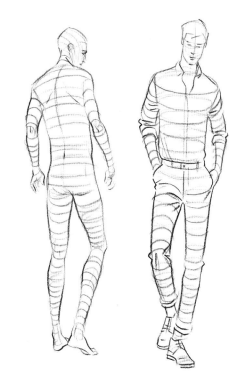

Figure 3.5 Cylindrical forms.

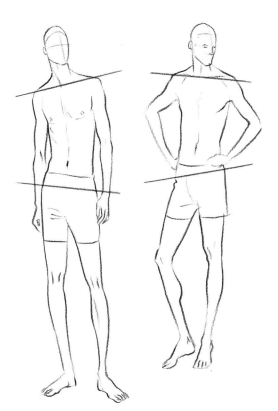

Figure 3.4 Action lines.

Figure 3.6 Cylindrical form in a sweater.

Figure 3.7 *Contrapposto*: Michelangelo's David.

CYLINDRICAL FORMS

Any movement of the body will affect the look of the garment. Even small shifts in the hips or shoulders will change how a garment appears. Analyzing and abstracting the figure into a series of cylinders, or bands of color, will not only help you to see and draw garment details—collars, armholes, waistlines, and sleeves—correctly, but will also aid in conveying the three-dimensional look of the clothed figure.

Contrapposto

Contrapposto is an Italian word that means counterpoise. A term popularized during the Italian Renaissance, counterpoise is the standing position of the body with the weight on one leg, and the shift in the body to counter this. As a result, the figure's hips and shoulders rest at opposite angles. Michelangelo's David is a perfect example of this stance.

This simple pose is a staple of fashion drawing, because it suggests movement, even though the figure is simply standing. The swing of the hip, and its weight-bearing leg, will have an upper body in counter-swing: The shoulders will tilt. Again, search for the center line of gravity. This subtle sense of movement is key in a fashion drawing. I would not underplay this movement. In a good fashion drawing, such action would be implied by tension lines drawn to suggest fabric being pulled by the body beneath the garment. We will examine this further in Chapter 4.

Walking Poses

Walking poses in fashion design sketches and illustrations have become more popular recently. This is due to the flood of catwalk photographs

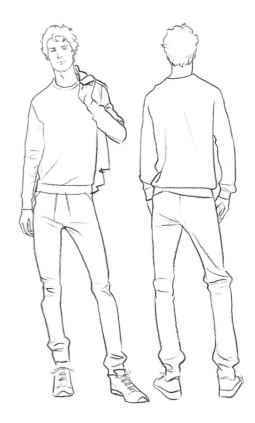

Figure 3.8 *Contrapposto* in a fashion figure.

of models walking that are now available online. We will discuss drawing from photographs in Chapter 4, but it is easy to see the appeal of these poses: They are dynamic and contemporary. Still, creating a convincing walking figure requires some thought.

Walking is a succession of steps that each involve balance and imbalance. A person walking is actually falling forward with a supporting leg. A whole range of subtle adjustments throughout the body are made in order to move: There is the swinging of the pelvis, the tilt of the shoulders, and even the position of the head over the weight-bearing foot. When walking, the body constantly shifts its weight from

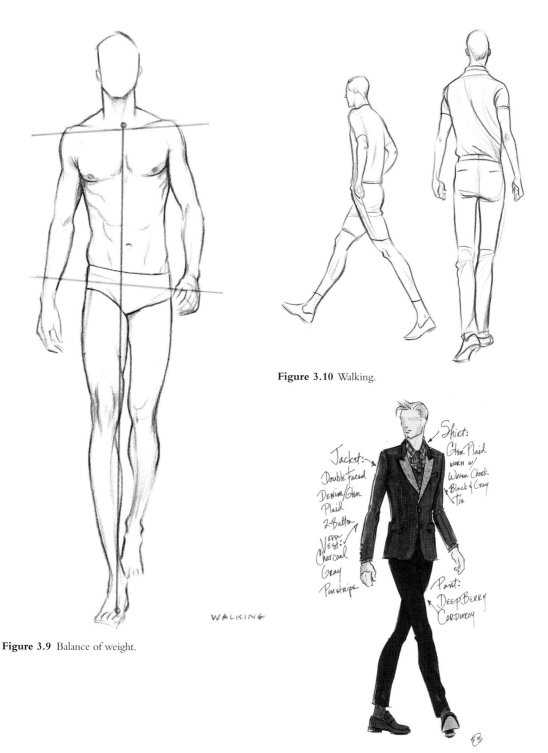

Figure 3.9 Balance of weight.

WALKING

Figure 3.10 Walking.

Jacket:
Double Faced
Denim/Glen
Plaid
2-Button

over
Vest:
Charcoal
Gray
Pinstripe

Shirt:
Glen Plaid
worn w/
Warm Check
Black & Gray
Tie

Pant:
Deep Berry
Corduroy

Figure 3.11 Renaldo Barnette.

Figure 3.12 Givenchy Spring 2001: Image courtesy of Eduard Erlikh.

Figure 3.13 Four Guys Walking: Image courtesy of Richard Haines.

one leg to the other, with the center of balance over the foot touching the ground. Usually, in a photo the leg is extended in front of the body, with the heel touching the ground. The leg at the back is either pushing off the ground with the toes or it is bent, with the lower leg foreshortened. The effort to remain upright and balanced while walking causes the arms to swing in order to balance the movement of the legs. To draw a figure that walks convincingly it is necessary to examine the photograph carefully. One must not only focus on the shape and contour of the figure but also be aware of the dynamic of the muscles being used and how they affect the clothing surrounding it. Look closely for the precise angle of the hips and shoulders and figure out where the center of gravity is. Remember the plumb line. Only careful observation can create a correctly drawn walking figure. A way of abstracting a photograph to draw from it will be investigated more closely in the next chapter.

Foreshortening–Sitting–Bending

Foreshortening refers to the distortion that happens when we draw a figure from an extreme point of view. It's what occurs when we view the figure, or any object, in perspective. An example would be a drawing of a man with his right arm outstretched in front of him, palm up, facing the viewer. The viewer would see his hand, and it would appear much larger than his head. Foreshortening is rarely seen in fashion illustrations. As stated earlier, anything that distracts from the immediate understanding of the garment can defeat the purpose of the drawing. That said, there are times when an interesting pose involving foreshortening can do more for a fashion drawing than a simple standing figure. The key, as always, is careful observation.

Foreshortening requires a basic understanding of perspective. This knowledge will allow the artist to see which parts of the body are thrust forward and which recede. Using the idea of transforming the figure into cylindrical shapes will help make the idea of perspective easier to understand and draw. Those parts of the subject nearest to us seem larger than those farther away. The best way to attempt such a pose is to study the model intently and draw what you see. You may need to constantly calibrate the effect of the body part closest to you, changing its size so that it doesn't look too forced or extreme. Keep in mind that this is a fashion drawing. If the foreshortening is too obvious, it will distract the viewer, so you may need to modify it. The key is to create a drawing or illustration that appears effortless. Anything that calls attention away from the communication of the garment is a distraction.

Figure 3.14 Hipster in a Parka. Illustration by author.

Figure 3.15 Image courtesy of Geoffry Gertz. geoffrygertz.com.

Figure 3.16 Top right: Bil Donovan; Bottom right: Clifford Faust; Bottom left: Mitchell Van Au; Top left: Author. Clifford Faust/Mitchell Van Au/Bil Donovan.

Seated figures are rare in fashion illustrations, and even rarer in fashion design sketches. Because the bottom half of the figure is distorted by foreshortening, the viewer cannot get a clear impression of the cut and length of the pants. Nevertheless, a seated figure can convey a wide variety of attitudes and can make an interesting and compelling graphic shape within a composition. In drawing a seated, or bending, figure, it is important to remember that the weight of the body is being supported by the buttocks, thighs, back hands, and elbows. Both the thighs and the buttocks will flatten due to gravity. Since the focus of the figure will be the upper body, care must be taken to make sure the head is drawn in proportion to the shoulders and upper torso. Even when drawing a sitting pose, you must think carefully about the center line of balance and the distribution of weight. The lower torso will be foreshortened, so a focused study of perspective and how the legs look in relation to the rest of the body is key.

Gestures

Before the invention of the high-speed camera and film, artists had to closely observe the quick movements of their subjects to capture how they walked, ran, jumped, or stretched. To record these actions, artists developed a kind of shorthand called **gesture drawing**. These sketches were a quick record of an action that would later be more fully developed in a finished illustration or painting. The point was to find the essence of the pose, to capture the feel of the model, in just a few lines. Today, the camera is an important tool for an artist, and, while helpful in capturing movement, the tradition of gesture drawing endures, because a good gesture drawing can capture the

essential energy of a pose in a way that a longer, more deliberative rendering might not.

The approach is straightforward: Since a typical pose for a gesture lasts no more than a minute or two, there is little time to do more than outline the proportion and movement of the subject. The technique is simple: Create a few flowing lines, random marks, scribbles, or doodles to capture the action of the pose with an economy of line. Step back. See the whole model. Put down on paper what you think you see. Gestures are to drawing what barre exercises are to ballet: a way of warming up and forcing the artist to quickly capture the essence of a model's pose. This exercise is an important tool to loosen up anyone who is used to using a pencil only for writing. While gestures are more often used with a live model, they can still be useful when drawing from a photograph. You only have to capture the movement of the model with a few free-flowing lines to get started. Spontaneity and concentration are all. It is also a way to challenge preconceived ideas of what a preliminary drawing should look like.

Figure 3.17 Gestures with wash.

Figure 3.18 Gestures.

Direct Sketching

Fashion designers have sketchbooks; these journals, or visual diaries, enable them to sketch ideas for collections, garment construction, or just an ad hoc collection of color and fabric. They are a valuable tool for a designer, a way of thinking on paper. A sketchbook serves as a visual record of the design development process. It organizes and archives design concepts and shows a prospective employer how one thinks creatively. Because such books reflect the style and personality of the designer, they tend to vary in size and presentation. Artists have sketchbooks too, but their books are a way of liberating themselves from the boundaries of the classroom or studio. Drawing from life forces the artist to record, in just a few lines, what he, or she, sees around them. It trains the eye and forces one to quickly put down, in as few lines as possible, what is of interest. It requires observation, speed, and knowing what to put down and, perhaps more importantly, what to leave out. It is one of the best ways to improve your drawing. Both books are important to have. Because neither sketchbook is meant for publication, artists and designers are free to scribble whatever they like. Go where you might be inspired or find interesting subjects: the subway, the park, restaurants, even department store windows—wherever there are people. Don't burden yourself by attempting a "finished" drawing. Whether you are a designer or illustrator, try to create sketches that stretch your technique and stimulate new ways of seeing and approaching the figure.

The *Croquis*

A *croquis* (pronounced "croakee") is another version of direct sketching. It is a term generally used by fashion designers and illustrators because the object being sketched is always a garment. A *croquis*, a French word, is a quick sketch of an item that will be drawn more carefully later. Because of this, it is necessary to draw accurately, observing and notating, so that one can redraw the garment with confidence. That means adding details like the right number of buttons and buttonholes, the length of the sleeves and seams. Note, too, the exact size and fit of the collar and lapels, and any other features unique to the garment. Adding brief written notes about the cut, fabric, color, and trim (belts, pockets, zippers, etc.) is also helpful. Typically, the garment being sketched is flat or on a mannequin; however, there might be occasions when you can sketch a garment on a model. In that case, you might use the same pose later in your finished drawing, so strict observation is a must. Once you have completed the sketch, go back for a second look and check to make sure you are as accurate as possible. Only then can you use these sketches as an aid for finished drawings later.

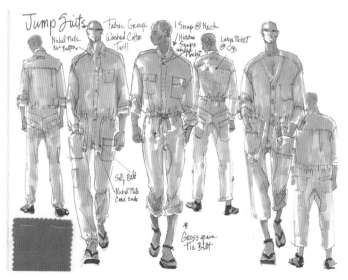

Figure 3.19 Image courtesy of Renaldo Barnette.

Figure 3.20 Image courtesy of Renaldo Barnette.

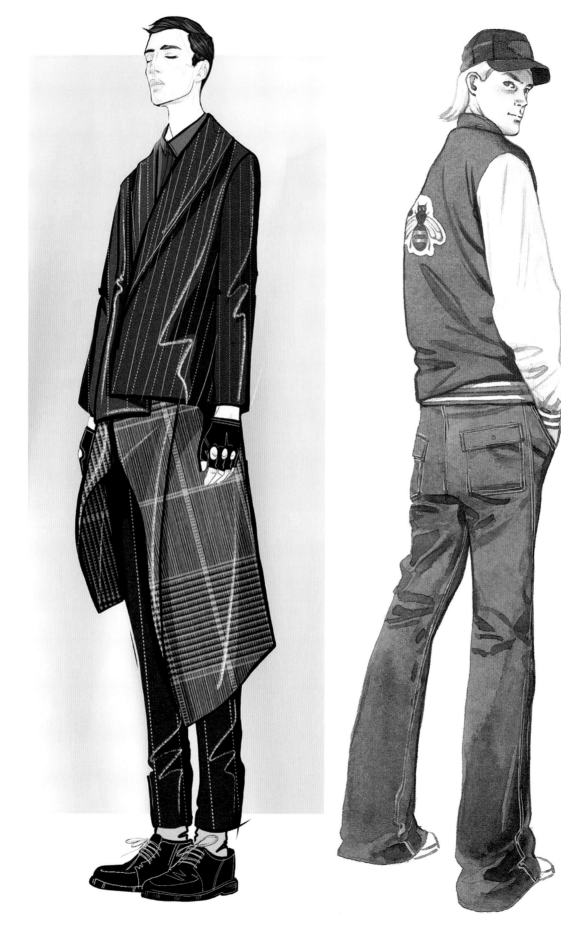

4

Drawing the Clothed Figure: Creating Dimension

Line and Contour

Shape, form, space, texture, value, color, and line. These elements of art are a kind of vocabulary, one that helps artists to both create and describe art: And line is perhaps the oldest, if not the most important, of these elements. From the ancient Paleolithic cave drawings in Lascaux, France, to the pen tool drawings of today's digital art, line continues to help us describe the world around us. Lines can have width, direction, texture, or force. They can be thick or thin, solid or fluid, delicate or harsh, curved or zigzagged. A line can be descriptive or abstract, and it can be both. Line is as fundamental to art, to drawing, as color is to paint, so we begin this chapter by exploring how to observe and draw the figure with line.

Figure 4.1 Illustration by Rosario Catrimini/Toulemonde. Illustration by Author.

To draw something is to try to understand it, and few things are more difficult to comprehend than the human body. The figure, after all, is a person. While we all know what a person looks like, putting that likeness on paper can be very challenging. Sometimes the subject is a live model, sometimes the figure is in a photograph. But in all cases, one is faced with a wealth of information: There is the hair, the mouth, the waist, the legs, a nose, shoulders, seams, and shadows. The list of characteristics goes on and on. Where does one begin?

We begin by abstracting the body. All images are abstractions, after all: A drawing is merely a record of our perceptions of the subject, not the actual subject itself. But here we're going to abstract, or deconstruct, the figure further by simplifying, in line, the figure before us. Paul Klee once said, "A line is a dot that went for a walk." In this chapter we will winnow the figure down to a manageable and easy-to-understand

Figure 4.2 Image courtesy of Carlos Aponte.

size. We start by drawing the form with a pencil, defining in a simple line, as accurately as we can, the entire figure from top to bottom. This is called contour drawing. Contour is a French word meaning outline. Think of this exercise as drawing a shadow in line: a way of conveying a three-dimensional figure in line without details. It is, in a sense, the drawing equivalent of "baby steps." By avoiding the more complicated aspects of the figure, and focusing on just the outline of the form, we can establish the height and width of the subject. Everything else is ignored. There is no inner drawing, just an outline.

This exercise is important because it increases your focusing skills and strengthens hand and eye coordination; this in turn helps you to draw more accurately what you see, instead of what you think you see. By paying particular attention to those negative shapes that are created by, say, a hand on a hip, or the space between the legs, we can slowly develop not only a more accurate drawing of an individual, but also a better understanding of the figure as a whole. The focus is on the overall view of the subject rather than details. There are no absolutely straight lines in nature. If you are carefully observing the model, or photograph, that will become obvious. In fact, one might argue that the only straight lines that exist are in technical drawings. It is the fluidity, deviance, and character of your line that will create an effective illusion in your drawing.

Directions

(1) Study the figure in the photograph. The pose is simple, and easy to understand. If you feel unsure about the proportions, you may, very lightly, draw a few guidelines, mapping out the angle of the

shoulders, center line, hips, arms, and legs. Then begin by using your pencil as an extension of your finger, tracing the outside of the model. (2) Start at the center of the head, working one side and then another, and back again. Try

Figure 4.3a Shape Within Shape.

Figure 4.3b Contour drawing.

drawing every bump, wrinkle, and crevice you see. You might discover that this is more difficult than it looks. That is because to accurately record the silhouette, you must continuously measure height against width, observing curves, straight lines, and negative shapes. **(3)** Using your pencil, measure height against width, constantly comparing your drawing with the photograph. This restrictive exercise will force you to really look at the figure, all the while concentrating on the edges of the model.

Shape Within Shape

The next exercise is a more complicated version of contour drawing; it is called Shape Within Shape. A common problem among beginning artists is their habit of drawing what they think they see, instead of drawing what is in front of them. In other words, their preconceptions of what a subject looks like often negatively affect their ability to observe accurately. This exercise not only focuses on the shapes that exist within the outlined figure; it also helps the artist see the figure without too much subjective distortion. By deconstructing and mapping the figure into a series of recognizable shapes, we can begin to build a fashion figure from top to bottom. For example, the hair, the shirt, the jacket, and the pants of the figure will each be rendered as enclosed shapes. Constantly measuring height against width—using a pencil as a rule of measurement—you must make sure that the shapes you put down are related in size and scale to the other shapes you have created. Be sure to close each shape before you go on to the next, so that by the end your drawing looks like a coloring book figure. In the previous chapters we discussed proportion, anatomy, balance, and

movement. Each of those topics, together with the exercises of this chapter, should inform all your drawings and help to create better fashion figures.

Directions

(1) Take a few moments to fully examine the model—observation is key here. Really look at the figure. Notice the many parts that make up the figure and try to mentally break up the model into different sections. At the end of the exercise, your drawing should resemble a paint-by-numbers page. **(2)** Using a pencil, determine the height of the figure, then lightly draw the center line and the balancing lines that help to define the angles of the shoulders and hips. **(3)** Begin the drawing by starting at the top of the head. Draw the shape of the hair as one enclosed shape. Then draw the face and neck as one enclosed shape, then the shape of the model's T-shirt as another shape, then the legs and arms. Be sure to close each shape before moving on. Pay particular attention to the negative shapes that are created by the arms and legs. The purpose of this exercise is to force you to look, and to select those shapes that best communicate what you see.

Drawing is mark-making, and every mark helps to describe the thing you're drawing. Make sure every line serves a purpose. Never use three lines when one line will do, and strive for accuracy. The purpose of these exercises is to develop your ability to see a figure in its disparate parts, and not be intimidated or overwhelmed by the whole figure. In other words, only by strict observation can you ignore your preconceptions and focus on what is actually in front of you.

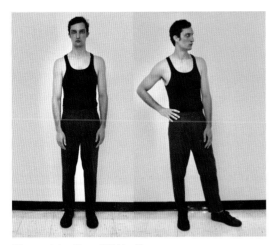

Figure 4.4a Shape Within Shape.

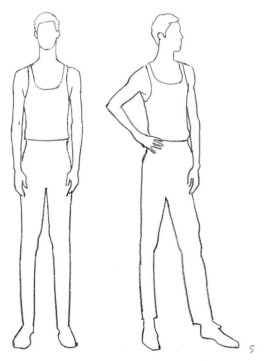

Figure 4.4b An example of Shape Within Shape.

Mass

Mass drawings in the wider art world are typically done in charcoal and are meant to represent the tonal values and solidity of a subject without line. Mass, within the context of this drawing exercise, refers to a figure rendered in tone or color without lines or edges. Again, the aim is to capture the form you see in front of you and not to rely on preconceived ideas of what you think the model is doing. It might be helpful to think of a figure rendered like this as a kind of shadow on paper. By using mass in this way, we are continuing to deconstruct the figure in terms of tonal shape. So far, we have examined the figure through line; now we are using the overall shape of the model as another way of simplifying the overwhelming information of the model. All the subtle curves, dips, crevices, and straight lines that you discovered in the previous exercise will now be translated into pure tone. Once you have completed the exercise, the next assignment will be to combine mass and line.

Directions

(1) Select photographs of three or four standing figures. Draw the figures on a horizontal page. Making sure that all the figures have the exact same proportion, create several figures in color marker using one tone to create a page of standing figures.

(2) Starting with a very light tonal shape; when finished, go over the sketch again, this time using different tones or colors for different parts of the body. Each of these individual shapes will look different, but when they're combined they will coalesce into a multi-tone figure.

(3) Combining mass and line.

Figure 4.5 Mass.

Figure 4.6 Illustration by author.

Combining Shape Within Shape and Mass

Combining Shape Within Shape and mass is the way most figurative artists paint. In a mass drawing or painting you're describing the figure through tone, or color, abstracting the figure by creating blocks of color. While for this exercise we will be using marker, one could just as easily use gouache, pastels, or even Photoshop.

Line Quality

Our focus up to this point has been how to confidently draw a male fashion figure. The exercises we have covered are the first step in bringing together all the necessary elements that would help bring that about: proportion, anatomy,

Figure 4.7 Image courtesy of George Gozum.

Figure 4.8

Figure 4.10 Finished marker figures using Shape Within Shape technique.

Figure 4.9 Example: Marker mass drawings.

balance, and shape. Still, when talking about line, it's worth mentioning how line should also be an expression of an artist's reaction to his subject. This is where line quality comes in. Line quality is a term heard often in fashion drawing. A good line drawing is one that exhibits a mix of draftsmanship, variety, character, and sensitivity. It is often a spontaneous result of an artist responding to a live model. In short, line quality has personality. Pressing hard on the pencil

Figure 4.11 Image courtesy of Bill Rancitelli.

will create a bold line that might convey a heavy fabric, or a shadow. A fine line from a brush, a marker, or a digital program might suggest transparency or simplicity—you decide. It is not always possible, particularly when drawing from a photograph, to demonstrate such nuance; nevertheless, one should try to imbue one's drawings with the kind of thought, commitment, and energy that helps to create a good drawing.

That means thinking about what the lines are meant to represent in your drawing: softness or bluntness, solidity or fragility, emphasis or minimization, or perhaps some combination of all of the above. Again, every mark you make should help to make clear what you mean to say.

The basic exercises that we have discussed so far will help you to create better and more nuanced fashion figures.

Figure 4.12 George Gozum, untitled drawing—2018.

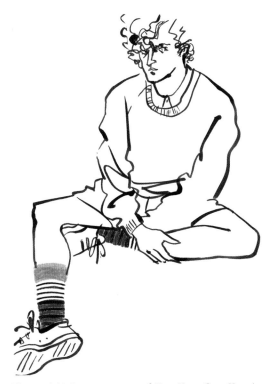

Figure 4.13 Image courtesy of Gary Kaye. Gary Kaye/ garykayeillustrations.com.

Figure 4.14 Richard Vyse.

Shadows and Tension Lines, Wrinkles, Folds, and Draping

Typically, shadows in a fashion illustration, and particularly in a design sketch, are kept to a minimum. Even in an illustration, too much ambiguity can make seeing the garment difficult. After all, the purpose of a fashion drawing is to explain and provoke interest, not to obscure or

Figure 4.15a Image courtesy of Leonard Cadiente. @bycadiente.

Figure 4.15b Image courtesy of Leonard Cadiente. @bycadiente.

hide. Nevertheless, there is still a place for selectively exaggerating dark and light values, to say nothing of adding subtle tonal changes, in a figure. It all depends on what the artist envisions, and what best highlights the salient features of the garment.

Shadows and highlights will look different depending on the fabric of a garment. For instance, the surface look of leather will be different than the shadows and highlights of velvet and wool. These differences will be explored later, in Chapter 6. But there are certain general ideas regarding shadows that can be examined now. What, for instance, is a tone?

A tone is the degree of value between light and dark. All colors have a value that can be brightened or darkened. When choosing a color to illustrate, most artists will select a medium tone to begin with. As the sketch develops, they can gradually add a darker tone of the color to the drawing—say, a darker shade of blue to a blue tone—or they may add a dark gray or even black to emphasize a shadow. Later still, they might leave the white of the paper exposed, or add white highlights to mimic the sheen of the fabric. Shadows and light cannot be separated from one another: the brighter the light, often the darker the shadow. This is particularly true of highly reflective fabrics like leather and silk.

Light Sources

Most of the light in fashion drawings is limited to four sources: light from above—ceiling lights or the sun—or lighting from the front, the left, or the right. As an artist and designer, you will decide the direction of the light source. Keep it simple. A simple light source is often all you will

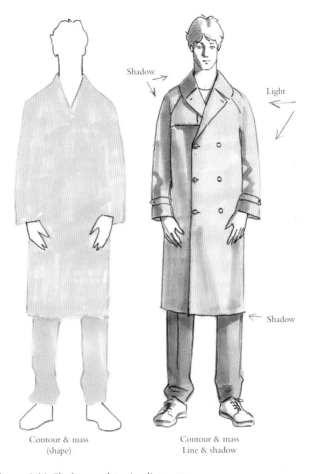

Shadow

Light

Shadow

Contour & mass
(shape)

Contour & mass
Line & shadow

Figure 4.16 Shadows and tension lines, etc.

need. Especially when drawing several figures on a page—say, a spread or design collection—keep the light source consistent for all your figures, whether from above, the left, or the right.

When drawing men's garments, there will almost always be shadows in certain places: under a hat or hood, under a lapel or collar, at the bottom of a jacket or coat, or when something is covered by another garment. Sometimes, the shadows that a menswear illustrator or designer creates have more to do with suggesting the body beneath the clothes than with lighting, which leads us to our next subject: folds and drapery.

Folds and Tension Lines

A garment on a hanger looks different from a garment on an actual body. A garment can even look different depending on how a figure stands or sits. Folds in a drawing help to explain what the body is doing beneath the clothes. One cannot accurately draw clothing on a figure without, in some way, indicating folds and tension lines. Not only do these lines suggest the body beneath the clothes, but they also help to explain the shape and structure of the garment. It might be easier to understand wrinkles and folds if we see example, let's say there are two identical suits; the shoulders are padded, the sleeves precisely set in, and the pants exactly measured, cut, and draped. However, depending upon the fabrics used, the two suits might look very different. That is because the folds and wrinkles will take on different forms depending on the texture and weight of the material. In short, the look and size of the folds are determined by how heavy the fabric is and what kind of material it is made of. A thin fabric like cotton jersey will have smaller folds, which will cause the material to bunch up. A thicker fabric like cotton velour will have fewer but larger folds. Hard, thin material like polished cotton, or canvas, will create stiffer and more angular wrinkles. Gravity will also affect the way a garment hangs on the body: Fabric weight, texture, volume, and length can alter the look of a garment on the figure.

The areas that typically have the most wrinkles are those areas where the fabric is being bunched, pinched, compressed, or pulled. Those areas on the figure would be the armpits, the elbows, the crotch, the knees, and the ankles. So depending upon the area of the body, the folds will have their own particular look. An example would be pinched folds in a shirt fanning out from the pinch point of the armpit.

A compressed fold would be the fabric being compressed under a bent arm, or leg, in denim. Another type of fold would be a spiral. We can see the spiral fold of a sweater, or shirt sleeve, when it is pushed up. The bulky folds at the knees of a pair of jeans have a soft zigzag quality when the figure is standing. They look like that because the fabric was pulled and stretched whenever the figure was moving or sitting, and when the fabric is relaxed, it sags. Learning to see wrinkles as an aid in describing a three-dimensional figure can only help your drawings,

Figure 4.17 Folds and tension lines: Image courtesy of Ryan McMenamy.

them as shapes that form hills and valleys. Try to imagine folds as the tops of hills that catch the light from above, while the valleys below are in shadow. These hills and valleys vary according to the height and width of the material.

Clothes are sort of a second skin, and men's garments, tailored suits in particular, are constructed to create a certain shape. For

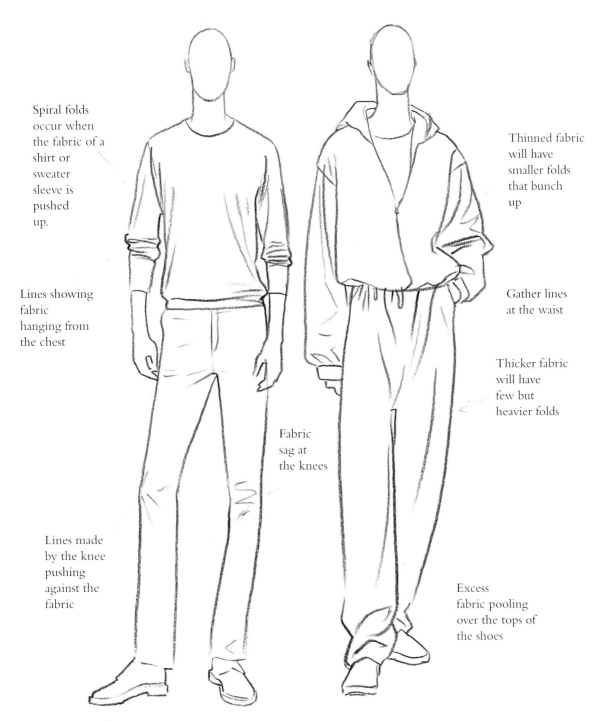

Spiral folds occur when the fabric of a shirt or sweater sleeve is pushed up.

Thinned fabric will have smaller folds that bunch up

Lines showing fabric hanging from the chest

Gather lines at the waist

Fabric sag at the knees

Thicker fabric will have few but heavier folds

Lines made by the knee pushing against the fabric

Excess fabric pooling over the tops of the shoes

Figure 4.18 Folds and tension lines.

but editing is a must. Too few wrinkles and folds and the figure will look like a stiff cardboard cutout, too many wrinkles and the man will look as though he slept in his clothes. Learn to see which few lines and folds will help describe the body beneath the fabric, and use such lines sparingly. And most importantly, remember: Any movement of the body will change the look of a garment. The closer the fit of a garment, the greater the effect the body will have on the garment.

TENSION LINES

Within the context of this book, tension lines are folds in the fabric that are being dramatically pulled and twisted by the body. On a loose-fitting T-shirt, the folds of the material will fall vertically because the excess cloth is being pulled by gravity. However, on someone wearing a tight T-shirt, the folds of the cloth will be horizontal because the fabric is being pulled or stretched across the body. These are tension lines. They are spare lines that emphasize the pull and direction of the material on the body. Used properly, they can help describe and underscore the movement of the body under the garment, even in tailored or heavier fabrics.

Figure 4.19 Folds and tension lines.

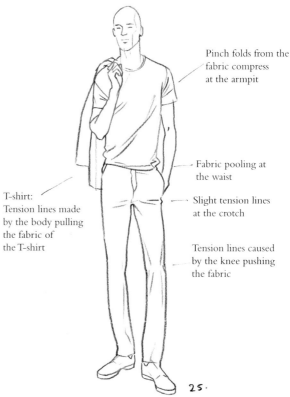

Pinch folds from the fabric compress at the armpit

Fabric pooling at the waist

Slight tension lines at the crotch

Tension lines caused by the knee pushing the fabric

T-shirt: Tension lines made by the body pulling the fabric of the T-shirt

25.

Figure 4.20 Tension lines.

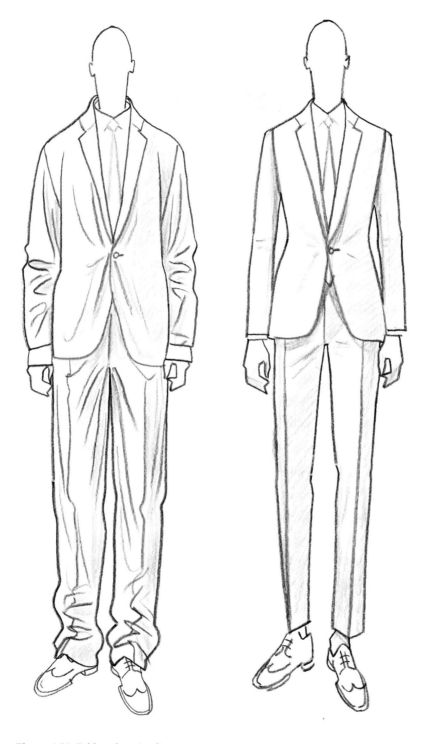

Figure 4.21 Folds and tension lines.

DRAPE

Draping is the way a fabric falls, or hangs, creating loose soft folds. This is the result of gravity. When cloth is draped, gravity will cause the fabric to bend, curve, and fold, flowing from one point to another. The size and heft of the folds will depend on the weight and texture of the fabric, and how it is manipulated. Though drapery is often seen in women's evening wear, it has long been a part of the history of menswear. Some past and current examples include the ancient Roman toga, the Southeast Asian sarong, and the Indian sari. Whether you are

Figure 4.23 Drape.

Figure 4.22 Drape.

Figure 4.24 Drape.

drawing drapery or folds, it is important to begin with the basic shape of the figure or garment. Working from a photograph or live model, look hard at the shapes and shadows in front of you. Be aware of the direction of the light source, and then start by lightly drawing the areas of light and dark. Notice the curvature of the folds and slowly build the tone of your shadows. Notice, too, the reflected light, and how close it is to the darkest shadows.

Line quality will also be important. A heavy fabric like wool might need a thicker line to suggest shadow and weight, while a lighter fabric like silk could be represented by a thinner line. Again, the look of the folds will depend on the fabric, lighting, and position of the body.

Figure 4.25 Illustration by Bill Rancitelli.

How to See and Draw from a Live Model, Photograph, or Template

DRAWING FROM A LIVE MODEL

When drawing from a live model, one must try to overcome two things: one's preconceptions about what one thinks and sees, and the natural fears and inhibitions concerning one's lack of skill. There is always a gap between the art we see around us, and the work we produce. At such times we always suffer by comparison. Try to remember that all artists were once beginners. One learns to draw by drawing, and observation and perseverance are the key. Look, and look again, try and try again. While few, if any, of your model drawings may be suitable for a portfolio presentation, the skills you develop through the practice, such as sustained concentration, observation, and problem solving, will contribute hugely to your draftsmanship.

Up to this point we've been carefully planning, step by step, how to approach and draw a male fashion figure. We discussed, in earlier chapters, the ideas of proportion, anatomy, balance, shape, and line. Each exercise has been, in a sense, another component in building a fashion figure. Now, informed by these concepts, one should be able to begin a drawing with some degree of confidence. As with all skills, repetition, practice, discipline, and patience will shape and refine your growth. Drawing from a model is an invaluable way of learning how to draw the figure.

Fashion illustration models, unlike magazine or runway models, come in all shapes and sizes. Traditionally, fashion models had to have certain proportions: They had to be tall, slim, and young. But while that may still be an industry standard,

Figure 4.26 Jose Gonzalez in NY—2019. Image Courtesy of George Gozum.

it's no longer the default choice. You can now choose a model that better fits a client's aesthetic, or one that reflects your own taste and vision. We are fast approaching a fashion world that embraces a wide spectrum of beauty, regardless of age, ethnicity, or body size. Character and style, and the ability to hold a pose, will always make up for a lack in ideal proportions. The important thing is to find a model who inspires you to draw the figure with confidence and skill. To that end, finding a model with whom you share a rapport can be extremely rewarding. If you can't hire a model because of the expense, try forming your own group. You can then pool your resources to hire a model, or ask a friend to model for you for free in exchange for a sketch. Most fashion design programs have drawing classes with live models, and many schools even have drop-in drawing sessions. The important thing is to continue practicing.

Professional models typically pose at twenty-minute intervals with five-minute breaks in-between. In a two-hour session the first twenty minutes are usually devoted to 10 two-minute poses for gestures. The next twenty minutes would be 4 five-minute poses. The rest of the session would then contain ten- and twenty-minute poses. It is helpful at the start of a session to have the model wear tank tops and shorts, or other body-revealing clothing, so one can more easily see the muscles and proportion of the model. This is particularly true for gestures, but it is also useful when you have a complicated pose involving layers of clothing that might obscure the body. Having a clearer idea of what the body is doing beneath the garment can only aid in the drawing of the clothed figure. You might have the model take a pose with a minimal amount of clothing, so you can see more clearly the muscles and stance of the figure, and then have the model take the same pose wearing clothing.

Figure 4.27 How to draw from a live model.

Figure 4.28 How to draw from a live model: Close-up.

Varying your model types, from slim and plus-size to young and older, is a good idea. Experimenting with different figure types can only help in your development as a fashion artist. Keep in mind that in the beginning phase of learning how to draw your aim is to be as faithful to the model as possible. However, as you develop more confidence and skill, you will learn to "reinvent" the model you are drawing, creating the ideal fashion figure you have in your head. This usually means focusing on those aspects of the model you find compelling and downplaying other parts. That's natural: It's called artistic license, and it is in some ways the very definition of what constitutes a fashion drawing. Absolute realism in a fashion drawing can be limiting and undesirable. A good fashion drawing involves a fair amount of editing, taking out certain things and accentuating others. Think of your drawing as an interpretation of what you see, instead of an exact record of the person.

Start the process in an area, a studio or classroom, with good lighting and a raised platform that elevates the model to just above eye level. A space where the model can change clothes privately is a good idea. A tilted desk or drawing board that allows you to take in both your page and the model in a single glance is a must. As for materials, choose inexpensive newsprint pads, or all-purpose paper, in a size that you find comfortable; 14" × 17" is a good size. Drawing pencils such as soft graphite (6B), charcoal, or 4B or higher drawing pencils are ideal. With a live model, begin by establishing the proportions of the model with a few light pencil lines. Start with the height of the figure—some nine heads high—and then mark off the anatomical landmarks that will help you to accurately describe the body, the head and neck, the upper and lower torso, legs, and then arms. Mark off the center line.

Measure the head against the width and length of the shoulders, torso, arms, and legs. Make sure the elbows are level with the waist and the wrist is level with the groin. Make sure the figure is standing upright by taking your pencil and finding the plumb line from the pit of the neck to the foot supporting the weight of the body. You have now created a kind of skeleton, one that will form the basis for your drawing. You can now use the Shape Within Shape method to flesh out the figure. Starting at the top of the head, draw the shape of the hair, the shape of the face and neck, the enclosed shape of the shirt, and so on. Once you've completed the figure, finish the drawing by adding the wrinkles, stress lines, and details—seams, buttons, etc.—of the garment.

There will be times when your drawings will not be completed by the end of the pose. In such cases you can have the model take the pose again, after a break, or use the unfinished drawing as a preliminary piece for another drawing. It is also likely that there will be corrections, erasures, and repetitions on the page. That is not unusual; in fact it's completely normal. Many artists have deliberately left such corrections in their drawings. These recorded mistakes are known as *pentimenti*, Italian for "repentance." They exist as a visual reminder of your thought process. They are meant to be a part of the creative process. Don't obsess about being finished or detailed. Every drawing should be, in a sense, an experiment. You can always use your drawings as a basis for more finished illustrations. But above all, use these sessions as an opportunity to learn more about yourself and the art of figure drawing. That would also include nude figure drawing. Fashion drawing with a live model entails not only drawing what you see, but also subtly changing the look and proportions of the model to conform to the current ideal.

Figure 4.29 How to draw from a live model: Ridge gestures.

Drawing a nude model in a life-drawing class forces us to look more intently at the human body without the artifice of fashion. Whether you are drawing a fashion figure or a nude live model, you are exercising a kind of exploration, a way of recording not only the subject in front of you, but also your idiosyncratic and individual reactions to the model.

EXAGGERATION IN FASHION ART

The previous chapters have focused on the mechanics of drawing, how to see the figure, and how to put it on paper. However, simply drawing a figure accurately does not make a good fashion illustration. Understanding the complex nature of drawing, the need for strict observation, technique, and skill, is merely one aspect of fashion drawing; there's also your personal reaction to what you are looking at, and how you choose to record and express your reaction. A drawing is a vehicle of communication, so as a fashion designer your drawing will explain something about the garment you hope to create, just as a fashion illustrator will describe their reaction to a finished garment. These drawings must depict specific clothing, and yet do so in a way that doesn't mimic a coldly clinical diagram. They must portray a fashionable figure in an appealing way. So, how does one go from a rigorously accurate drawing to a fabulous and captivating fashion illustration? In a word, exaggeration.

To exaggerate something is to magnify and emphasize it. In this context it is to reinterpret an article of clothing, making it more attractive, and more compelling, by exaggerating a salient aspect of the outfit, or figure, for dramatic effect. That might mean creating unconventional figures and garment proportions, or it might mean artwork that is more highly stylized and experimental. Your choice of media or pose will no doubt be considered, but simply recording the facts of a garment will not be enough for a good fashion drawing. That is because exaggeration is a large part of fashion. Knowing what to exaggerate or highlight can be the difference between an image of someone merely wearing clothing, and someone wearing fashion. The difference may be a subtle one, but to the trained eye it is the difference between an amateur and a professional. One of the easiest ways to improve a fashion figure is by exaggerating contrasts, either of line, texture, shapes, or proportions. Here are several examples.

Figure 4.30 Exaggeration in fashion art—Robert Melendez. Images courtesy of Fashion Institute of Technology SUNY FIT Library of Special Collections and College Archives.

Figure 4.31 Exaggeration in fashion art.

Figure 4.32 Exaggeration in fashion art—Cody Cannon.

Figure 4.33 Exaggeration in fashion art—Carlos Aponte.

DEVELOPING A KNOWLEDGE OF FASHION

Developing one's imagination is central to an artist; it is, in fact, a never-ending process. Not only do we look around us, but we also look inside of us. Like everyone else, that means we're constantly being influenced by the world around us, and our reaction to what we see and hear. The difference is that we record our reactions through art. We may start with talent, but it is

our education that polishes and refines what is innate. And by education, I don't mean just what we learn in school, but also what we choose to seek out in art and fashion. Museums, art galleries, and fashion shows are crucial sources of inspiration; so are fashion publications, digital magazines, Instagram, and other online sites. For fashion designers or illustrators, these can not only keep them informed but can also inspire and influence. Being influenced by artists you admire is right and natural, if such inspiration doesn't descend into plagiarism. But even then, your education does not end. In short, to create a good fashion illustration, one must know something about fashion. Reading books on fashion designers and fashion artists and familiarizing yourself with the history of fashion can only increase your understanding of your profession. A measure of curiosity, in all things, is essential, but critical thinking is a must. What are the trends in menswear? What is THE look in current male fashion? How do the current social and political movements inform menswear, if at all? What is the current relationship between art and fashion? If you can talk intelligently about fashion, then your opinion becomes an informed and authoritative opinion, one that can then be translated into your art and design. Sensibility and awareness, married with skill, are what makes a successful fashion illustration.

DRAWING FROM A PHOTOGRAPH

Photographs are curated images. They are pictures in which the decisions about the subject matter: Lighting, clothing, color, environment, and theme have already been decided. In other words, what we're looking at in a fashion photograph is a set of secondhand perceptions made by a fashion editor, a photographer, and a team of professionals. This is why most artists, and art schools, prize live drawing with a model over photography. Since all drawing is a form of seeing, drawing from life is a way of developing your own distinctive way of expressing what you see. Fashion drawing is no exception.

Nevertheless, almost every fashion artist and designer has, at one time or another, used a photograph as a reference source. And since many designers and illustrators rarely have a model to draw from, it is important to know

how to look at a photo, and how to then translate it into a drawing.

First, find a photograph that is easy to understand. You should be able to quickly see the angle of the shoulders and hips, which leg is bearing the weight of the body, and the relative proportions of the figure. Choose an image with a head-to-toe figure. Make sure the photograph is taken slightly straight on, or slightly above, and avoid exaggerated and distorted images due to a forced perspective. Using a sheet of tracing paper, trace with a pencil over the photograph using the Shape Within Shape method. This mapping technique will force you to see only the shapes of the posed figure without the distracting details of hair, folds, shadows, and clothing. However, do NOT trace the photograph and use that as a drawing. Your objective is to reinterpret the photograph as a stylized fashion figure, not to slavishly copy it. A traced figure will not only look amateurish and out of proportion; it will also look like … a tracing. So, use the tracing only as a guide to help you clearly see the relative shapes that the model makes.

Setting both the photograph and your finished tracing off to the side, you can begin your drawing as you would with a live model, using both the photograph and the tracing as a guide. The tracing should help you see the different shapes of the figure so you can more closely draw what is in the photo. The photo will give you all the details that you will need to further describe the garment. You will then lightly sketch a skeleton of the figure in the photo, before drawing the figure using the Shape Within Shape method. Remember to think about proportion, and where to lengthen the figure. Using the photo as the basis for your design sketch, you can now change or alter the garment to resemble more closely what you have in mind. Later, add details

Figure 4.34 Drawing from a photograph.

like shadows, wrinkles, and garment details to further enhance your drawing. Remember to edit your drawings: Better too few lines than too many.

Note: When working from a photograph, remember to consider whether the image is copyrighted or is royalty-free. When using a photo from a website, and particularly if your image will be published, it is a good idea to change the image so that it bears no resemblance to the original.

DRAWING ON A TEMPLATE

Templates are very popular with some designers, and it's easy to see why. Templates, sometimes called *croquis* templates, or flat templates, are black-and-white drawings of unclothed fashion figures printed on paper. For a designer unsure about their drawing skills, or with a heavy workload, sketching quick designs on a prefabricated figure is a plus. However, I think it best to create your own template.

Assignment

Your drawing will be of a man standing straight and facing forward with his arms at his sides. A static image like a photograph might be a good idea. You can use the image on the following page or find another one online. (1) Begin with a light underdrawing of a figure, marking off the most important body landmarks: the head, neck, shoulders, upper torso, lower torso, legs, and arms. It is at this stage that you should pay particular attention to the proportions of your figure. What type of template do you want? A template that will be used for flats is different from a template that will be used as the basis for a fashion figure. A template figure for flats will have proportions

that will be less elongated and much more realistic (an example of that type of flat can be found in Chapter 6).

(2) A template for a working fashion design sketch will have the typical "nine heads" look. Start with the head. Once you have the head and the neck, draw the plumb or center line. This should start at the base of the neck and end at the bottom of the feet. If your figure is balanced and standing straight, the plumb line should end between the feet. If you like, you can use a ruler to measure off the major landmarks. Using the examples shown here, redraw the figure, changing the proportions—or keeping them—as you see fit. Depending upon your personal taste, or the wishes of a client, your figure's proportions can be as traditional or as stylized as needed. However, it is important to remember that whatever proportion you choose, all your figures must have the same consistent proportion. Remember that an illustrated design collection should represent clothes that are clearly created for the same body type.

THE ROUGH DRAWING AND THE FINISHED DRAWING

Every artist at some time reworks a drawing. Sometimes a quick sketch is perfect. It has wit and energy and explains the garment perfectly. And sometimes a drawing simply needs more work. While drawing from life affords an immediate and spontaneous response to a model, most fashion designers and illustrators will rarely have an opportunity to draw from life. Even if they do, time, money, and other circumstances may limit an artist's ability to use a model. In that case, whether using a model or a photograph, a rough sketch can serve as a preliminary stage, the first step in a process toward a more finished illustration or sketch.

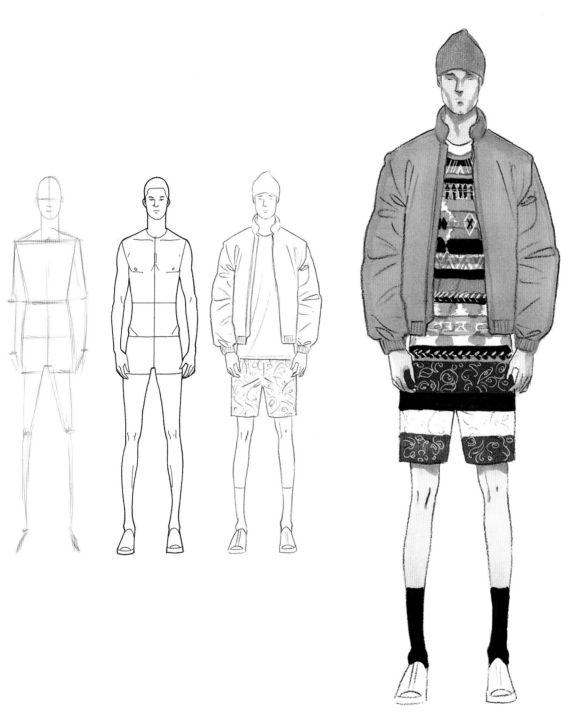

Figure 4.35 Drawing from a template.

Figure 4.36 Step by step, drawing from a template.

It might help to think of rough drawings as a discovery technique. Like a sculptor carving a figure out of a block of stone, a preparatory drawing can be the beginning of the gradual evolution of a piece or the basis for a more refined and polished illustration. The key here is a rigorous critique of your rough sketch, with you asking the question: How can I make my drawing better?

One can start by examining the drawing and answering some key questions: Are the proportions and anatomy correct? Is the figure balanced and standing properly? Are the shapes of the garments clear? Do the folds and shadows add depth and dimension to the figure, or are they haphazard scribbles? Be honest with yourself. Some of these questions are easy to answer after a careful examination of the sketch, and some require more focused attention. Because this is the first stage, now would be the time to experiment with the sketch, to perhaps exaggerate the proportions or stylize the figure. Better to go too far at this stage than to play it safe. You can always tone down the approach or change your mind later. Also, when we work closely on a piece, we often become blind to our mistakes. We're so used to seeing the drawing that we can't see what might be obvious to others. We need some distance. Many artists will put a drawing aside for a day or two, coming back to it later.

One way to view your drawing with fresh eyes is to hold your sketch in front of a mirror. This reversed view will show you whether your drawing is lacking symmetry, or is out of proportion, or is just misshapen. Another tool is to draw your rough on a sheet of tracing paper, and then turn it over to see the drawing on the other side. Like the reflection in a mirror, you'll be able to see what your drawing looks like with fresh eyes. Then, by correcting your drawing with a red pencil on the reversed side, you can flip the paper over again and see your corrected red lines. You can then edit

and redraw your rough with your red lines as a guide. Many illustrators and designers draw their roughs on tracing paper, only to later transfer the rough to the paper they intend to use as a finish.

Learn to develop a clear-eyed evaluation of your work. This will require a certain degree of humility. One of the most important lessons to be learned as an artist is how our art might look stacked up against the work of other artists. Being too sure of the value of your work can be just as harmful as too little confidence; both can hamper genuine development, because the lessons we learn from our mistakes help us develop into the skilled artists and designers we aspire to be. Lastly, be careful not to "overwork" your drawing with too many lines, shadows, or media. The best fashion drawings look effortless, not labored over. Strict realism is not interpreting fashion. Try to interpret what you see with as much imagination and skill as possible.

How Can I Make My Drawing Better? A Check List

Consistency is the hallmark of professionalism. To be able to produce, on demand, the same level of technical skill and problem solving, repeatably, is what separates the amateur from the professional. This is particularly true with commercial art. Creative and design directors expect you to reproduce similar artwork to what they have seen in your portfolio, or on social media. If your figures change in proportion from drawing to drawing, or if they appear off balance, or obviously anatomically wrong, your work will be seen as hopelessly amateurish and not worth their time. So, before you submit yourself to the cold criticism of the outside world it's best to make sure that your work can stand up to review. To that end, become your own best critic. Try to have some critical distance when it comes to your work. That means being aware of your limitations, and yet constantly testing them. Too much self-criticism can be inhibiting and counter-productive, while too little can lead to an unearned smugness. Try to strike a healthy balance. Keep in mind that this is part of a life-long process. Start by really looking at your work.

First, if you have a group of figures, make sure that all your figures have the same proportions. This is especially true if this is a design page and you have more than two figures on a page. Their height, shoulders, waist, knees, and feet should all align. Because fashion art can vary from realistic to hyper-stylized, a great deal of leeway is given to personal expression in fashion art. Even so, a consistent look and feel will make it easier to accept a unique style, while a constant varying of style and proportion in figure after figure may suggest inexperience. Second, all figures should be standing with their feet flat on the same floor, and not floating or tipping off balance. Remember the plumb line. And third, your figures should look as though they belong together, not just in terms of proportion, but in the sense that they look vaguely related to one another. This is especially true if you are illustrating a design collection. Even without an illustrated environment, by creating a group of figures that appear somewhat related to one another, you are creating a narrative (see figure 4.39). Some other suggestions: Look at your drawings as objectively as you can. Are your figures too short or too tall? Is that figure anatomically correct? How do the individual abstract shapes of the figure look in relation to one another? Is the torso too short in relation to the legs? Are the arms too long? Is the head too big? Look at your rough—you should always start with a rough drawing—and your source material, whether a live model or a photograph, and look, and look again, and redraw, and redraw again. Only when you have a sound and well-drawn rough can you then go on to a finish.

Figure 4.37 Movement.

Creating a Picture

FUNDAMENTALS OF DESIGN

Just about every painting or illustration you have ever seen began as a plan. The artist or designer had to work out where to place the figure, or figures, on the page. This arrangement of the figure, along with other elements on the page, is called a layout or composition. Think of it as a sort of blueprint, a process that involves using space, line, color, and texture to create a harmonious picture. Simply put, a layout, or composition, is the careful placement or arrangement of visual elements on a blank page that create a sort of balance. Balance in a work of art is creating order out of chaos. It is a planned approach to a painting or illustration involving an arrangement of parts to create a whole. These parts, or elements, include things like movement, emphasis, contrast, symmetry, pattern, and scale. A successful composition draws the viewer in, subtly leading the viewer's eye across an illustration so that a single point of interest immediately tells the story. There are often contrasting areas of light and dark, and whether the arrangement is symmetrical or asymmetrical, the overall look is well balanced. Just as simply drawing a clothed figure on a page isn't a fashion drawing, arbitrarily placing a figure on a blank page isn't a composition.

A good composition requires thought and planning. The basic principles of design will always be present in all good compositions. A good layout can enhance a mediocre illustration, while a bad layout can detract and undermine even an excellent drawing. Always think about the placement of the figure on the page. Obviously, drawing a single figure on a page is relatively simple, but adding one or two more figures means working out how the figures will relate to one another. In that case, it is helpful to do a few thumbnail sketches to get a quick sense of the effect of the figures and their relationship to one another. In other words, consider whether the figures would work well in an environment—in a room or on a sidewalk, or against a single blank background. One might use a large figure in the foreground as a point of interest or play with contrasting sizes and colors to create a more dynamic composition. Poses overlapping one another might also create some visual contrast. As with all art, experimentation is key. There are several important elements that go into composition:

Movement: Creating movement or rhythm in a composition might mean the flow of an ink brush, the repetition of an element—lines, shapes, or colors—or the placement of figures inside a picture that will lead and guide the viewer's eye to certain areas (see figures 4.37, 4.38 and 4.44).

Focus, or **emphasis**, is usually the focal point of the picture, the figure or object that is predominate. When other elements compliment the focal point, the design is harmonious (see figure 4.39).

Contrast is created when two elements are opposites: black against white, thick against thin, or big against small. Contrast allows one to emphasize a figure or element on a page in contrast to another. Simple positive and negative space is an example of contrast (see figures 4.41 and 4.2).

Figure 4.38 Illustration by Alvin Pimsler. Image courtesy of Fashion Institute of Technology SUNY FIT Library of Special Collections and College Archives.

Balance occurs when you place a large element on one side of your page and a smaller element on the other side. It is distributing the visual weight on the page so that both halves of the design are still somehow visually equal (see figure 4.40).

Symmetrical and **asymmetrical compositions:** A symmetrical composition is one in which the two elements on the page are evenly spaced and mirrored. They are identical parts on opposite sides of an imaginary dividing line. An asymmetrical composition can be any arrangement where the two main elements are not equal and are unbalanced but might give the illusion of equally distributed weight (see figures 4.43 and 4.47).

Pattern, in the graphic or compositional sense, is a repetition of lines, shapes, or colors in an illustration that creates a visual consistency. Much like a rhythm in music, a repeated element can create a visual movement that allows the eye to travel (see figure 4.45).

Scale often works in conjunction with contrast. Placing a larger exaggerated figure within a slightly smaller graphic environment can create a dynamic composition, and vice versa. Scale can also help to suggest an environment within the picture frame (see figure 4.46).

Figure 4.39 Size matters. Image Courtesy of Gary Kaye. Gary Kaye / view-publications.com.

Figure 4.40 Jasjyot Singh Hans. Image originally created for *LAAB* magazine #2 EAT/SHIT. Curated by Ronald Wimberly, published by Beehive Press.

Figure 4.41 Contrast. Ryan McMenamy..

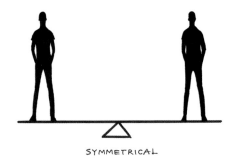

SYMMETRICAL

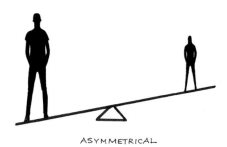

ASYMMETRICAL

Figure 4.43 Symmetry.

Figure 4.42 Contrast.

Figure 4.44 Pattern. Richard Kilroy.

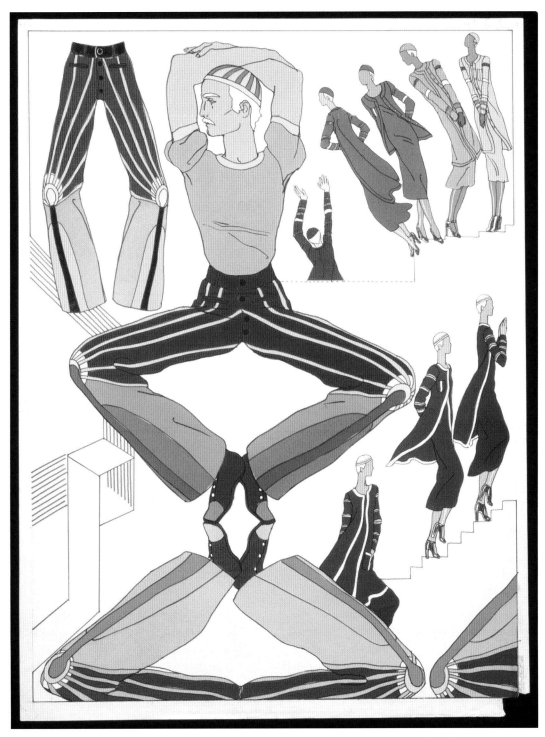

Figure 4.45 Antonio. *Søen* magazine, Juan Ramos wearing Stephen Burrows, 1969. Pen and Cello-Tak on paper. The Estate & Archives of Antonio Lopez and Juan Ramos.

Figure 4.46 Scale. Robert Melendez.

Figure 4.47 Symmetry. Richard Haines.

To create an illustration with a single figure is relatively simple, particularly if there are no other elements involved. However, once you add two or more figures, you should probably consider the arrangement of the figures and their relationship to one another. One way to do that is to create thumbnail sketches, small quick sketches using light and dark shapes that indicate the placement of the figures. These sketches should help you see how contrasting forms and tones shape the overall design, and whether there is an easy flow with the elements guiding the eye. When grouping figures with a single background, the perspective of the figures should relate to the background: They should look as if they were all standing, or sitting, on the same plane. If there is a dominant figure, it should be used as an anchor that unites the other figures in the composition. Again, planning is key.

DRAWING IN PERSPECTIVE

For most of history, pictorial art was rendered in flat stylized images. Artists back then could not convincingly convey a three-dimensional world. Finally, in 1415, Filippo Brunelleschi, an Italian Renaissance architect, changed that by creating a method for delineating form and distance. This method is called perspective, and it helped artists to better represent a three-dimensional reality on a two-dimensional surface. It is this realistic impression of depth that creates the illusion of distance, dimension, and form.

From a fashion artist's point of view, an academic approach like perspective might not seem necessary in a fashion drawing. But I believe a general theory of perspective is necessary for anyone who believes in good drawing. One can begin to understand the theory by simply looking straight ahead at an imaginary horizontal line on a wall. Don't look up, or down, just straight. The line should be at the same level as your eyes, whether you're standing or sitting. Drawing a line on a paper representing this view would be described as eye level. This line establishes a horizon line. All objects drawn at that eye level will look flat, anything drawn above or below will show a third dimension. Now, add a dot at the center of the line. This is the vanishing point. You now have one-point perspective. Imagine a set of railroad tracks that start as two parallel lines; as they recede into the distance, the lines converge as they meet at the vanishing point. In one-point perspective there is only one vanishing point, and it is centered at eye level. All perspective lines will converge at this one point. All horizontal lines will be parallel to the horizon line.

A two-point perspective is useful for drawing a cube. (1) First, establish a right-hand vanishing point, and a left-hand vanishing point on the horizon line (or eye level). The sides of the cube will diminish according to their distance from the vanishing point. (2) Then draw a vertical line (the perpendicular axis) to create the angle nearest you. (3) Draw the converging lines starting from the vanishing points. There are one-, two-, and three-point perspectives. Each perspective is named for

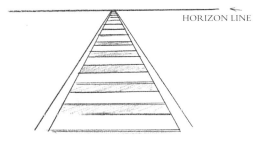

Figure 4.48 One-point perspective.

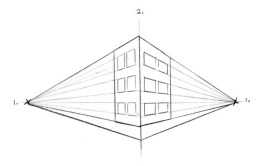

Figure 4.49 Two-point perspective.

the number of vantage points in a drawing. All forms of linear perspective involve a horizon line, vanishing points, and lines of perspective that advance or recede from the vanishing points. For accuracy's sake, one should use a ruler, a T-square, and a triangle. While perspective is not generally used in fashion illustration, a basic understanding can help a designer or artist when composing a page with several figures, or when a figure exists within an environment.

5

Drawing the Garment: Details

The Basics: Suit and Blazer

A good fashion illustration is more than just a drawing of a garment. To be successful, the artwork must persuade the viewer that this article of clothing is meaningful. It must attract a prospective buyer, and so whatever unique qualities exist within the garment must be accentuated. This is where the artist comes in. Look at the garment, study it. What are the qualities that make this garment appealing? How is it made? What is the fabric like, how does it move? What is the most interesting aspect of the garment? Is it luxurious, or practical? Conservative, or hip? What is the silhouette? What is the fit? To achieve your objective, you must have a clear understanding of the construction of the garment, and how it looks on the figure. This is always important when drawing any garment, but particularly so when the subject is tailored clothing.

When one thinks of traditional menswear, one inevitably thinks of tailored suits. But what is meant by tailoring? Tailoring is the art of designing, cutting, fitting, and sewing garments to conform to the body. The word "tailor" comes from the French word *tailler*, meaning "to cut." As mentioned in the Introduction, menswear in general, and tailored clothing in particular, is largely derived from military uniforms and the equestrian clothing of the upper classes. The earliest tailors appeared during the Middle Ages as linen armorers. These men—and they were always men—created padded linen garments that were worn under the chain mail of armored knights to protect the wearer from chafing.

From that time on, a master tailor would have an apprentice: an aspiring tailor who would learn the art of tailoring from close observation. Apprentices would learn their craft by molding woolen cloth in the shape of a body. Once they had mastered that skill, they would then add different elements, creating a variety of effects and styles that would showcase their skill.

Figure 5.1 Details: Drawing the garment.

Because of this method of teaching, there were no written manuals on tailoring until 1796. There were, of course, guilds and brotherhoods, but this scarcity of experienced tailors helps to explain why, historically, only the aristocracy or the very rich could afford custom-made clothing. It wasn't until the Industrial Revolution, and the growing purchasing power it brought to the middle class, that ready-made and custom-made clothing was made more affordable, and therefore more widely available.

This period—roughly from 1820 to 1878—is often described as the Golden Age of tailoring. Now a garment no longer needed ornamentation or other finery to be elegant: Simplicity of cut and fit was the new ideal. It was during this time that the profession's reputation soared. Master tailors in London and Paris had the sorts of brilliant careers that would have been unthinkable just a few decades before. And all of this was due to the rapid evolution in tailoring techniques. Measuring became more precise, with the introduction of measuring tapes (or "inch tapes"), and undesirable folds and crooked lines soon disappeared. It was during this period that the three-piece suit emerged. While similar, it was not yet the modern silhouette that we recognize—that suit didn't appear until 1920.

The gradual mass production of garments, due to the invention of the sewing machine, along with new forms of marketing, made the appearance and availability of ready-made suits inevitable. Still, differences in quality remained; many would still purchase a bespoke suit from a tailor, or made-to-measure, if they could afford it. London's Savile Row was still the gold standard in men's fashion. By the second half of the 19th century, the invasion of ready-made suits was complete: They dominated the market. By 1910, with the introduction of lighter suit fabrics,

Figure 5.2 Illustration by the author.

summer or "Palm Beach" suits become popular in the US. Since that time, the tailored suit has evolved over the years into a near ubiquitous garment for the modern professional man.

A suit, whether custom-made or off-the-rack, is a precisely cut and sewn garment designed to fit the body. A "bespoke" suit is a made-to-measure garment for a specific client. It is called a bespoke suit because it is a garment that is "spoken for" and not for sale to the public. It is also a suit with the kind of precise tailoring details that are rarely, if ever, seen in mass-produced clothing. While there are a wide variety of jackets and coats, the basic construction of a tailored jacket has remained nearly the same for well over 200 years.

When drawing a tailored garment, it is important to remember a few things. (1) Keep your lines and shapes clean and sharp. Too many lines will create a badly wrinkled suit; too few will give your figure a stiff, cardboard look. Practice restraint when drawing a suit, adding only those folds that hint at the body beneath the fabric—editing is everything here. (2) Make sure your drawing of a suit, particularly when drawing a front view, is balanced and symmetrical; when you draw one side of the garment, make sure the lapels, collar gorge, pockets, etc., on the other side are mirrored. (3) Pay particular attention to the details of the construction, the look of the shoulders, the position and length of the sleeves, the weight of the fabric, shape of lapels, pockets, seams, buttons, and buttonholes, and all of the details that make up the particular look of that garment.

DRAWING A SINGLE-BREASTED JACKET

To begin, it is important to note the details and construction of a blazer. The shoulder lines will have a slight slope from the top of the collar to the top of the armhole. The top collar is a separate piece which is connected to the lapel and goes around the neck. It falls onto the shoulder, and then the upper chest. The line of the lapel in a drawing should be straight and precise, with a slight shadow above the top button that suggests the roll of the fabric. There will also be slight shadows under the top collar and lapel. Note that men's garments close left over right (in a drawing that would be right over left). Notice, too,

Figure 5.3 Illustration by the author.

the silhouette and placement of the collar, lapels, buttons, and pockets. In finishing a drawing, rendering the various seams and top stitching throughout the garment can add to the overall detailed look of the jacket.

Figure 5.4a Illustration by the author.

Figure 5.4b Image courtesy of Jusun Lee. Jusun Lee.

Figure 5.4c

Figure 5.4d Image courtesy of Francisco J. Cortés.

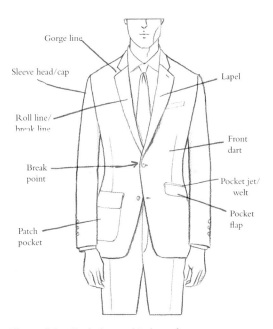

Gorge line

Sleeve head/cap

Lapel

Roll line/
break line

Front
dart

Break
point

Pocket jet/
welt

Pocket
flap

Patch
pocket

Figure 5.5a Single-breasted jacket—front.

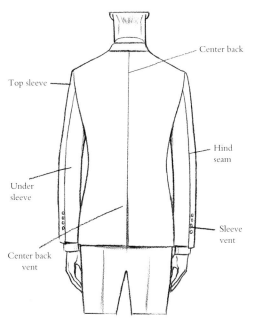

Center back

Top sleeve

Hind
seam

Under
sleeve

Sleeve
vent

Center back
vent

Figure 5.5b Single-breasted jacket—back.

In a design sketch the seams and top stitching are usually rendered with a dotted or broken line. In a fashion illustration the seams can be done with an unbroken line. Remember, the details, proportion, fit, and fabric of a garment distinguish it from any other period. Drawing clothing details precisely is key to successfully rendering a garment.

Draw the shoulder lines sloping from the neck to the top of the shoulders. Where the deltoid would meet, draw a slightly curved line indicating the seam of the armhole. This line should suggest the roundness of the shoulder. Then draw the top collar as a separate piece joining the lapel.

Figure 5.6 Illustration by the author.

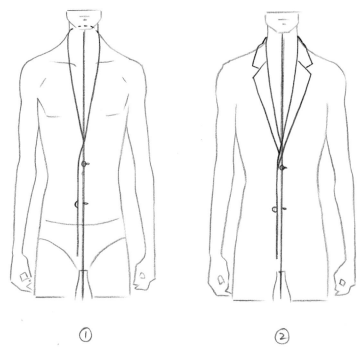

Figure 5.7a How to draw a single-breasted jacket.

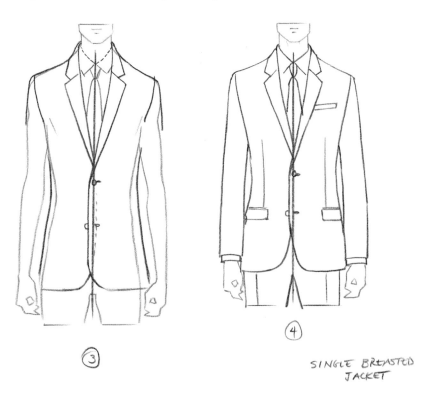

SINGLE BREASTED
JACKET

Figure 5.7b How to draw a single-breasted jacket.

Now that you have a nearly completed blazer, add the sleeves. Keep the arms slightly bent, with some space between the arms and the sides of the jacket. This will allow the viewer to see how tapered the waist is. Add sleeve buttons. Pay close attention to the fit and look of the jacket on a figure. Though jacket styles and silhouettes may change, typically a suit jacket should always fit, but not too tightly. Notice how the collar sits around the neck, and the exact fit of the shoulders and armholes. There are different types of shoulders, so be clear about which one you are illustrating. Observe the break point—this is where the lapels fold over from the inside of a jacket. It is the central pivot point of a jacket—how high or low is it? Make sure you add the necessary details to the jacket; darts, side seams, and pockets. Above all, try to recreate the overall effect of the suit by choosing the correct pose or stance. The way the figure stands can communicate how the garment should feel, and who ideally would wear it.

Figure 5.8 Illustration by the author.

Drawing a Double-Breasted Jacket

Like the single-breasted jacket, begin with a figure as an underdrawing. Place a sheet of tracing paper on top. Begin by creating a center front line. Draw a curved line from the left from around the neck to the center line. From the right, draw a line to the center line. Both lines should meet at a point slightly below the chest. Extend the line to the left of the center line midway between the center line and the edge of the body, ending slightly above the waist. This line should be parallel to the center line. Drop this line to about wrist level.

Now draw the peaked lapels, making sure they are symmetrical. Draw the top collar attached to the lapels. Add the shoulder lines and the armholes. Draw the sleeves. Add three rows of buttons equidistant from the center line. The first two buttons are slightly below the chest, the second two buttons are at the waist, and the third row is at the hip. Be sure to add buttonholes.

Figure 5.10 How to draw a double-breasted jacket.

Figure 5.9 Illustration by the author.

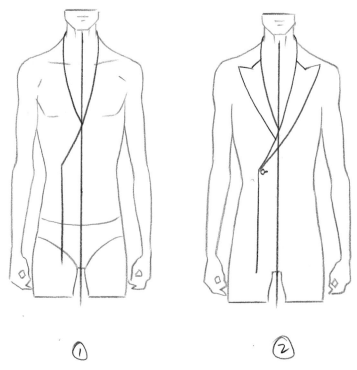

Figure 5.11a Drawing a double-breasted jacket, steps 1 and 2.

Figure 5.11b Drawing a double-breasted jacket, steps 3 and 4.

Figure 5.12 Modern—2019. Image courtesy of George Gozum.

Figure 5.13 Illustration by the author.

ILLUSTRATED GLOSSARY OF JACKETS AND BLAZERS

Two-button double-breasted jacket with set-in sleeves and notch collar

Fitted three-button jacket with set-in sleeves and notch collar

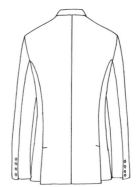

Jacket with two short side vents at the back

Two-button jacket with peak lapels

Fitted four-button jacket with set-in sleeves

Norfolk jacket

Safari jacket

Fitted single-button jacket with with shawl collar

Jacket with yoke and notch lapels

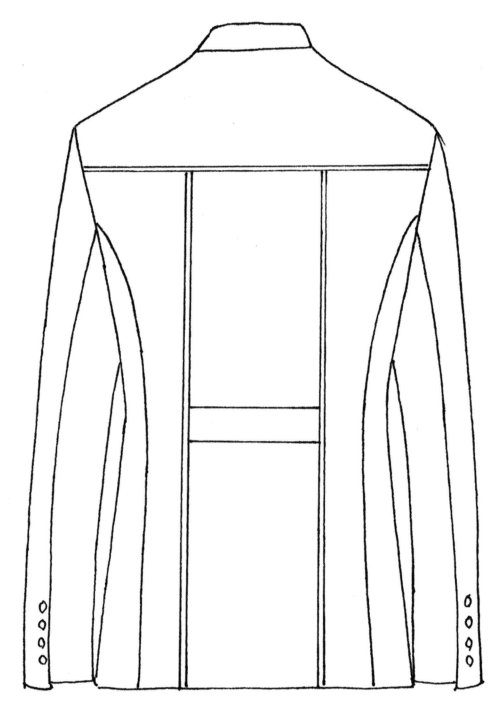

Norfolk jacket with rear view

Figure 5.14 Jacket glossary.

TROUSERS

It is only 200 years since men's trousers began to develop into the garment we recognize today. The earliest incarnation of trousers were breeches, which were pants that ended just below the knee. They had a button-fly and were often buttoned at the knee (today, breeches, also called jodhpurs, are tight-fitting trousers that are generally worn for horse riding). By the 1820s, the pantaloon had replaced breeches; pantaloons were slim trousers with foot straps and a notched instep. Gradually, the foot straps of the pantaloons disappeared, and the final evolution of the pant was complete.

By the mid-19th century, men's trousers began to resemble the modern pant more closely. These had a button-fly front instead of the "falls" (a front panel that buttoned on the sides), and trouser cuffs, which were created to lift the trouser hem above the dirt. Soon, trouser creases were made fashionable by the Prince of Wales (later Edward VII). By the beginning of the 20th century, the fly-front creased trouser became a staple of menswear.

DRAWING TROUSERS

As with drawing jackets, one should begin by sketching a center front line; this line will represent the rise in a pant. A rise is the length between the waistband and the center of the crotch seam. There are two types of rises: a low rise and a high rise. Pants with a high rise will sit a little higher in relation to the waist, a low rise will sit lower on the body (e.g., harem pants, dhotis, or parachute pants, as worn by MC Hammer).

Trousers, or pants, vary in width and length. Shorter pants ending above the ankle are described as "cropped." Longer-length pants will have what is known as "breaks." A break is a fold at the lowest ends of the pants where the fabric reaches the shoe. There are quarter-breaks, half-breaks, and full breaks. A break is not to be confused with a crease.

A crease is a traditional look in semi-formal and formal trousers. Typically, a sharp crease is ironed down the center of a pair of pants, adding a crisp sophisticated look. In a drawing, a crease is represented by a simple straight line that runs vertically down the front of a pant, breaking only as the crease hits the top of the shoe.

It might help to imagine a drawing of trousers as a series of circles. The first circle is the waist, the second, the hips, and the third, the legs. The trouser legs are cylindrical, starting out wider at the upper thigh, then, generally, narrowing toward the hems. On wide pants the excess fabric will create a tension line caused by a slight pull from the hip. Tight-fitting pants like skinny jeans will more closely show the muscles of the legs.

Begin by establishing the waist and then the length and width of the pant legs. Does the waist have a high or low waist? Are the pants close-fitting or baggy, cropped or tapered? How heavy or light is the fabric, and what do the folds and tension lines look like? And finally, what are the garment details and embellishments that make the pants unique? As always, observation is key.

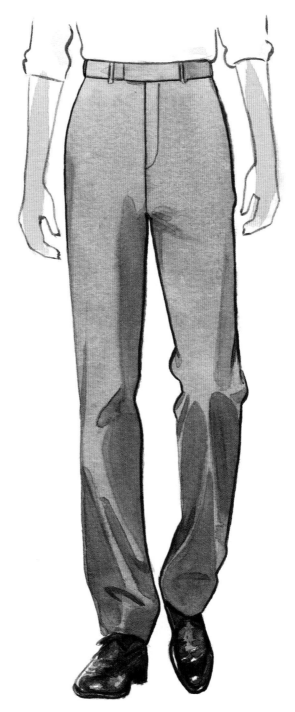

Figure 5.15 Trousers.

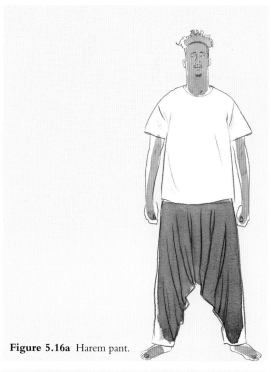

Figure 5.16a Harem pant.

Figure 5.16c Wide leg.

Figure 5.16b Creased pant.

Figure 5.16d Slim fit.

Figure 5.17 Loretta Tedeschi-Cuoco Zouave Pant. Image courtesy of Loretta Tedeschi-Cuoco 2020.

Figure 5.18 Illustration by the author.

THE SHIRT

The shirt as we know it is a descendant of the long tunic, a universal menswear staple for hundreds of years. In the 17th century, European men wore the abbreviated tunic, or shirt, as a kind of underwear; it was worn to protect the outer garments from sweat and dirt. By the 18th century the shirt made an outward appearance in an incarnation that more closely resembled the modern-day garment, only with ruffles, jabots, and elaborate collars. Detachable collars and cuffs appeared around 1828. These collars and cuffs, made from cloth and paper, were created so that they could be worn every day without changing the shirt. The popularity of these ready-made parts was due to the difficulty and expense of laundering shirts. Clean white shirts signaled one's social status and professionalism. The demand for detachable collars and cuffs remained steady until the late 1920s.

Today there are as many different types of shirts as one can imagine—dress shirts, sport shirts, sweatshirts, T-shirts—but they all follow the same basic pattern of a collar, a main body, and two sleeves. As in all fashion drawing, the details are all-important.

DRAWING A BASIC SHIRT

Although there are many different types of shirts, perhaps the most common, other than the T-shirt, is the dress shirt. The dress shirt remains an important staple in a modern man's wardrobe. The basic structure is simple: It has a collar, cuffs, yoke, stitching, buttons, side seams, gussets, armholes, and hemline. As with all garments, a clear understanding of the individual elements and how they work together can only aid your drawing.

As before, begin with an unclothed figure (cropped or full figure), and place a sheet of tracing paper over the drawing. Begin by drawing a center front line. Once done, draw a spread collar. Draw the band collar as though it was wrapped around the neck, with no gaps. Using the center front line as a guide, make sure both sides of the collar are symmetrical. Sketch in the shoulder and the overall silhouette of the shirt. Add the cuffs and sleeves. Add a few short lines where the inside of the elbow would be, to indicate the occasional compression of the fabric. Finally, sketch in the placket. This should lie on top of the center front line. Draw the buttons on top of the center front line, making sure that the buttons are equidistant from one another. As with the drawing of jackets, symmetry in a shirt is important.

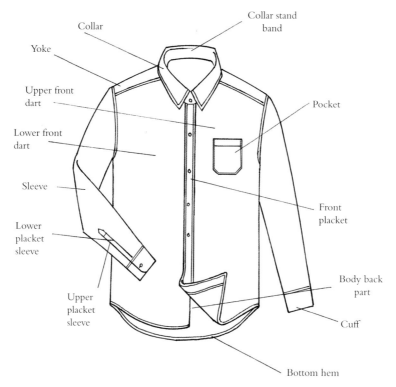

Figure 5.19a Shirt front.

Collar stand band

Collar

Yoke

Upper front dart

Lower front dart

Sleeve

Lower placket sleeve

Upper placket sleeve

Pocket

Front placket

Body back part

Cuff

Bottom hem

Figure 5.19b Shirt back.

Figure 5.20 The shirt on a figure.

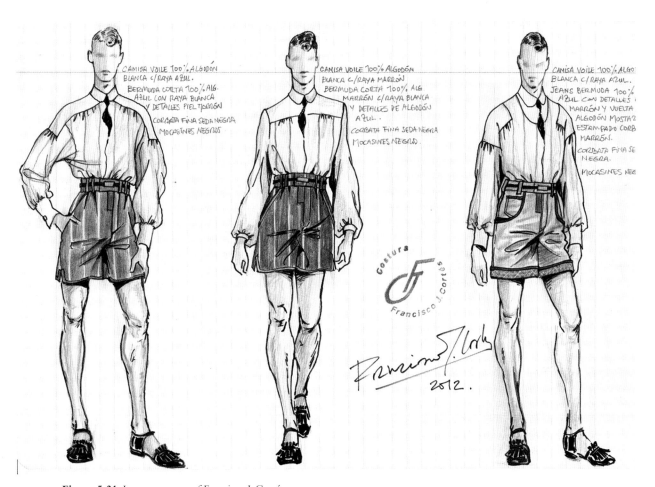

CAMISA VOILE 100% ALGODÓN
BLANCA C/RAYA AZUL.
BERMUDA CORTA 100% ALG.
AZUL CON RAYA BLANCA
Y DETALLES PIEL TOSTADO
CORBATA FINA SEDA NEGRA
MOCASINES NEGROS.

CAMISA VOILE 100% ALGODÓN
BLANCA C/RAYA MARRÓN
BERMUDA CORTA 100% ALG
MARRÓN C/RAYA BLANCA
Y DETALLES DE ALGODÓN
AZUL.
CORBATA FINA SEDA NEGRA
MOCASINES NEGROS.

CAMISA VOILE 100% ALGO
BLANCA C/RAYA AZUL.
JEANS BERMUDA 100%
AZUL CON DETALLES
MARRÓN Y VUELTA
ALGODÓN MOSTAZ
ESTAMPADO CORB
MARRÓN.
CORBATA FINA SE
NEGRA
MOCASINES NEG

Costura
Francisco J. Cortés

2012.

Figure 5.21 Image courtesy of Francisco J. Cortés.

ILLUSTRATED GLOSSARY OF SHIRT COLLARS AND CUFFS

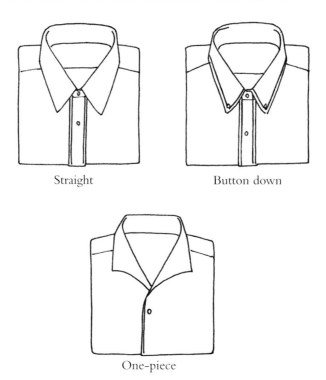

Straight   Button down

One-piece

Figure 5.22a Shirt collars.

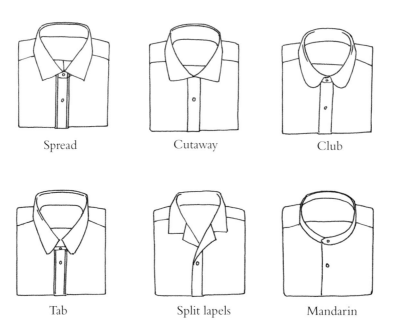

Spread   Cutaway   Club

Tab   Split lapels   Mandarin

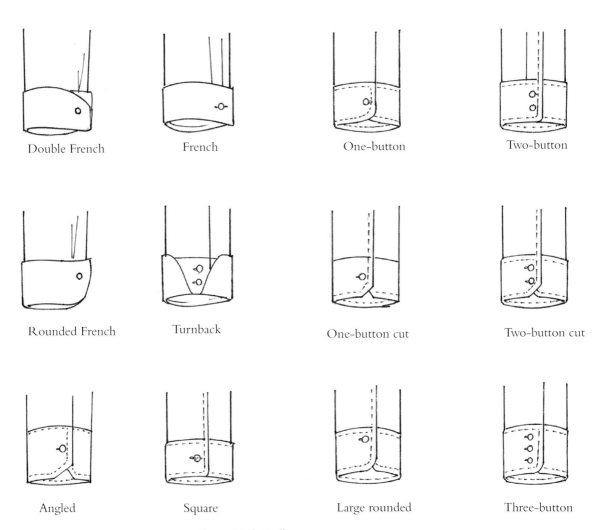

Double French   French   One-button   Two-button

Rounded French   Turnback   One-button cut   Two-button cut

Angled   Square   Large rounded   Three-button

Figure 5.22b Cuffs.

Outerwear

It was in mid-18th-century France that the modern cloth coat made its appearance, and like almost all menswear, it owed its existence to the military. By the next century, there were different coats for different times of the day. Formal evening wear for men consisted of tailcoats, cutaway coats, and morning coats. Daywear styles included frock coats, sack coats, and town coats. Bad weather usually meant Inverness capes. However, around 1835 all of that changed with the sudden inexplicable popularity of the overcoat. The overcoat was neither a cloak nor a tunic. It had no horizontal seams, no pleats under the arms, and was made from a coarse broadcloth. It was, in fact, a simple waistless sack. Double-breasted with many buttons and two large pockets, it resembled a lumpy oversized peacoat. Still, if nothing else, it kept the wearer warm.

After being adopted by Dandies and men of the upper classes, the overcoat inevitably became high fashion. These particular coats were better fitted, worn close to the body, and made from an array of fine fabrics. But as the overcoat became more popular with the working classes, its silhouette changed, becoming looser and more comfortable. With the introduction of mass production, and the availability of affordable ready-made clothing, it became a kind of uniform, worn by the rabble and bourgeoisie alike. In that sense, one could argue that this was the origin of the modern men's coat. The overcoat remained popular until the First World War, its ungainly size and bulk contributing to its slow demise. While the peacoat is the closest descendant of the 19th-century overcoat, a wide selection of men's coats have replaced it.

While any garment worn over any attire is technically outerwear, there are countless variations of men's outerwear: peacoats, trench coats, chesterfields, flight jackets, motorcycle jackets, Polo coats, puff jackets, denim jackets, and on and on. The fabrics that are usually used to make outerwear range from cashmere and mohair to worsted wools, flannels, tweeds, velvet, and assorted man-made fabrics. Often the linings of these garments are satin, silk, or cotton.

DRAWING A COAT

The best way to emphasize the overall shape and design details of a coat is to draw it facing forward, with the coat closed. Of course, if there are important design details inside the coat, or on the sides, or in the back, your choice of poses should reflect that. Make sure you can visualize and understand the body beneath the coat. Then begin by first drawing the overall shape. You can do this by drawing the coat in two separate parts, the left side then the right, or the top and bottom, if there is a defined waist.

Figure 5.23 Double-breasted topcoat. Illustration by author.

Figure 5.24 "Overcoat and bulldog" in the style of the Apparel Arts. Illustration by author.

Figure 5.25 River Island Menswear: Mengjie Di.

Figure 5.26 Image courtesy of Gary Kaye. Gary Kaye /garykayeillustrations.com.

ILLUSTRATED GLOSSARY OF OUTERWEAR

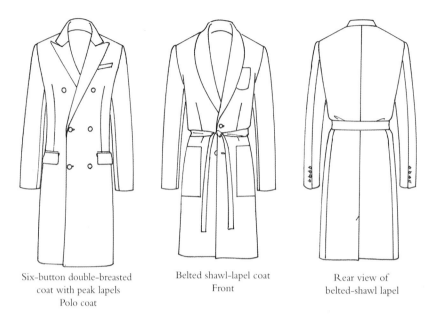

Six-button double-breasted
coat with peak lapels
Polo coat

Belted shawl-lapel coat
Front

Rear view of
belted-shawl lapel

Figure 5.27

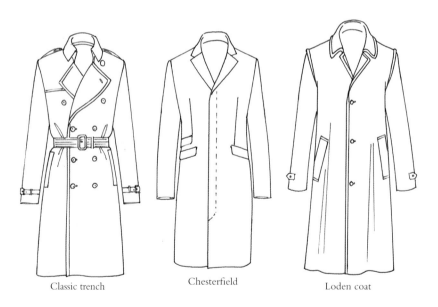

Classic trench

Chesterfield

Loden coat

Single-breasted
trench

Duffle coat

Belted coat

Barracuda jacket

Bomber jacket

Varsity jacket

Pea coat

Nautical style coat
Front

Nautical style
coat Back

Aviator shearling
jacket

Motorcycle jacket

Biker jacket

Parka with
hood

Raglan car coat

Belted coat with
sherung collar

Denim jacket

Puffy coat

Knits and Sweaters

Prior to 1918, an Englishman, and therefore any man interested in fashion, was always seen in a coat, suit, and tie. A certain unvarying formality was the mark of a Victorian gentleman. The starched collar, tight jackets, and ramrod posture epitomized the sort of sober and mature man that was ideal at the time. The post-war years of the 1920s changed all that. A new generation came along with its own ideas about masculine dress and modernity. Now athleticism, informality, and youth became ideal. This is apparent with the introduction of the sweater. Where before there was the stiff vest or jacket, now there was the soft jersey pullover, or the Fair Isle vest. From the 1920s on, knitwear and sweaters become synonymous with modernism. Introduced as comfortable and less formal wear, the pullover, or the fisherman's knit, soon became a staple of everyday menswear, reflecting both the growing desire for comfort and simplicity in menswear and the slow, but steady, casualization of menswear.

There are two basic types of knitwear: fine and heavy knits. Heavy knits would include cable sweaters, cardigans, certain crewneck and V-neck sweaters, and sweatshirts. Light knits would include jerseys, turtlenecks, light polo shirts, tank tops, and T-shirts. Knits can be hand-sewn or cut and sewn machine-knitted.

Figure 5.28 Image courtesy of Eduard Erlikh.

Figure 5.29 Image courtesy of Gary Kaye. Gary Kaye / garykayeillustrations.com.

Figure 5.30 Illustration by author.

Figure 5.31 Illustration by author.

Figure 5.32 Image courtesy of Brian Lane.

Figure 5.33 Illustration by author.

ILLUSTRATED GLOSSARY OF KNITS

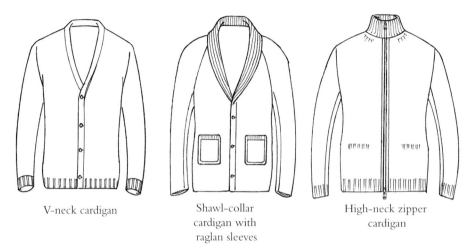

V-neck cardigan

Shawl-collar cardigan with raglan sleeves

High-neck zipper cardigan

Figure 5.34

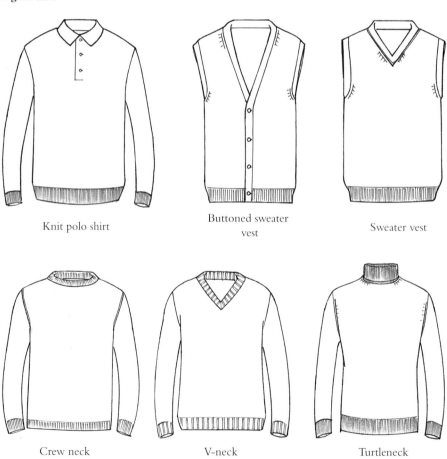

Knit polo shirt

Buttoned sweater vest

Sweater vest

Crew neck

V-neck

Turtleneck

Aran sweater

Cable-knit sweater

Norwegian Sweater

Raglan hooded
sweatshirt

Hooded zipper
sweatshirt

Hooded pullover
sweatshirt

Sportswear

Sportswear has traditionally meant those garments made for the affluent, who could afford clothing specially made for their leisure activities. Typically, this meant aristocratic pursuits like horseback riding, tennis, golf, badminton, and bicycling. These activities had become less class-bound by the early 20th century, due to an ever-growing affluent middle class. By this time, almost everyone played some sort of sport, from bowling and swimming to skiing and basketball. By the 1980s, gyms had become popular, and clothes were now designed and made strictly for the gym. But it was the rise of urban hip-hop-driven streetwear that really popularized sportswear. Casual became cool. Sweatshirts, hoodies, polo shirts, sweatpants, sneakers, baseball caps, and tracksuits slowly became standard items in a contemporary man's wardrobe.

This represented a fundamental shift in men's fashion. Technological breakthroughs in hi-tech fabrics and cutting made possible low-maintenance garments that didn't require constant pressing or dry cleaning. Clothes that were originally created for physical exertion are now worn because they're comfortable and require less effort. The suit and tie of an office worker hasn't disappeared; he's merely added a hoodie under his sports jacket, and sneakers with his trousers.

Sportswear today represents the casualization of menswear and the growing influence of Millennials. Sportswear, activewear, and "athleisure," are now three different categories of sports clothing. Sportswear refers to garments designed specifically for sports, while activewear is a recent section of menswear that refers to clothing that has been designed almost exclusively for exercising. Athleisure is a hybrid form of sportswear typically worn in settings other than the gym. Such garments can now be worn at home, while shopping, at the workplace, or in other casual places. The trend supposedly began in women's yoga classes; the clothes, such as yoga pants, tights, leggings, shorts, tees, and sneakers, are made for light exercise and walking. Seen as the next step in sportswear, athleisure represents yet another step in the idea of sportswear as comfort dress.

Critics may argue that the next fashion accessories might be a blanket and pillow, but is comfort not the ultimate luxury? Contemporary examples of activewear include, but are not limited to, tracksuits, T-shirts, shorts (spandex or Lycra), sweatpants, and sweatshirts; Sportswear includes not only items like jeans, pullovers, and shirt jackets, but also specialized garments for sports like swimming, skiing, basketball, riding, tennis, golf, and ice skating.

Wearing sportswear is no longer just casual fashion, but high fashion. By the early 21st century, sportswear like tracksuits, sneakers, and hoodies have become as ubiquitous as denim jeans. Some popular sportswear companies include Rocawear, FUBU, 10.Deep, Supreme, Stussy, Noah, and the sportswear behemoths Adidas, New Balance, and Nike, to name a few.

Figure 5.35 Image courtesy of Mitchell Van Au 2021.

Figure 5.36 Illustration by author.

Figure 5.37a Image courtesy of Ricola Wille.

Figure 5.37b Image courtesy of Rosario Catrimi.

Figure 5.37d Image courtesy of Loretta Tedeschi-Cuoco 2020.

Figure 5.37c Illustration by author.

DENIM JEANS

Fashion is about change. From season to season, year in and year out, the fashion industry creates a demand for a new look. This change is based on the requirements of fashion production and profit. Denim, however, is an exception to the rule. For the last eighty years, the look of denim jeans has remained remarkably constant. The blue jean—copper rivets on pocket corners, five pockets—whether in indigo stretch fabric or denim twill, is the same on the streets of Taiwan as on the roads of Soweto or in the classrooms of New York. As such, the denim jean has become the most common, and therefore the most recognizable, form of sportswear in the world.

Denim's ubiquity is a result of several factors: the growth and purchasing power of the youth market, the ever-expanding influence of American popular culture, the relaxation of dress codes, the casualization of the workplace, and the ever-evolving response of manufacturers to consumer demand.

In the mid-1960s jeans became a symbol of an emerging counter-culture. Back then, the young were advised to wear their jeans in a bathtub so they would shrink to the shape of the wearer. Afterwards, the jeans would abrade and fray in a way that suggested a life span. The holes, rips, and tears would further "personalize" the garment. After repeated wearing, the cloth would become softer and more comfortable. It would become a deeply personal artifact, the wear and tear of the denim reflecting the character of the owner. It is this unique relationship of wearer and garment that the denim business is trying to replicate through pre-sold distressing. If a well-worn pair of jeans can suggest a life, then the denim industry is offering, through distressed denim, a kind of manufactured nostalgia. It is this notion of clothes with a traditional life span artificially aged, aside from the look and feel of the fabric, that has such appeal for buyers of distressed denim.

"Denim" and "jean" were originally two different fabrics. Denim was a more durable twill, usually dyed in indigo and crossed with an undyed, white weft, while jean—a similar fabric first produced in Genoa, Italy, around the same period—was a woven fabric with two dyed threads. After a while, the two fabrics, often used in the same production of goods requiring sturdy cloth, became interchangeable. What we call denim has had many names: One version was called *drill*, a coarser fabric that at one time was called "blue drillin's," a duck or canvas. Dungaree—a name still in use as a synonym for denim—apparently descends from an even coarser, brown fabric originating in Dungaree, a village in present-day Mumbai (Bombay), India. A dungaree cloth, heavy and dense like canvas, was often used in tents and sails. Seamen were assumed to have recycled the torn and tattered ends of the sail into uniforms, including bell-bottoms. From the beginning, denim was prized for its toughness and durability. The popular blue jean that we know today is the achievement of two men: Levi Strauss, a San Francisco dry goods supplier, and Jacob Davis, a struggling tailor. While working on a horse blanket, Davis realized that the copper rivets he used for straps could also be used to reinforce seams and pants pockets. Seeing the potential in selling durable work pants, but not eager to invest yet again in a patent fee, Davis wrote to the wholesaler and offered him half interest in exchange for the price of a patent. After examining several sample pairs of the pants, Strauss agreed, and after several rejections from the patent office, Levi Strauss & Co. was awarded a patent number on May 20, 1873.

For the next 100 years, denim jeans slowly but steadily became a mainstay of American sportswear. In the 1920s jeans became associated with the country's sudden interest in everything western. With a little help from Hollywood, cowboys and gunslingers suddenly became popular icons representing rugged individualism. By the 1930s department stores began to market and sell women's jeans. During the war years of the 1940s, women began to wear jeans in the workplace in order to take on the jobs left vacant by enlisted men. Jeans now became a symbol of practicality, "up-to-dateness," and almost patriotism. And by the 1950s the growing cultural power of the American teenager turned the denim jean into a symbol of youth and non-conformity.

Today, not just denim jeans, but denim jackets, coats, and shirts have become a near global presence, existing in almost every country in the world. Denim jeans are as American as Coca-Cola and apple pie, and yet this garment has an almost universal appeal.

Even though they are a part of fashion, denim jeans resist the continual changes of fashion. They represent both high and low fashion. Each generation seeks to define itself in opposition to the previous generation by wearing blue jeans in a provocative way.

There are many different types of denim—dark rinse, light blue, and even white. Distressed denim might be faded, bleached, stonewashed, frayed, ripped, cut, or torn. As with regular trousers, the fit and fabric of denim jeans will determine its look.

Figure 5.38 Illustration by author.

BASE COLOR

PRISMA COLOR BLACK

WHITE PENCIL HIGHLIGHT

DENIM

Figure 5.39 Illustration by author.

CAMISA POPELÍN/ALGODÓN 100%.
BL/GRIS/AZUL.
JEANS AZUL LAVADO CON
DETALLES EN MARRÓN
Y VUELTA EN ALGODÓN
ROSA ESTAMPADO
CORBATA FUCSIA.

CORBATA FINA
SEDA NEGRA

MOCASINES
NEGRO.

Francisco J. Corts
2012.

Figure 5.40 Image courtesy of Francisco J. Cortés.

Accessories: Hats, Shoes, and Bags

HATS

There was a time, as recent as the late 1950s, when a gentleman was only half-dressed if he wasn't wearing a hat. Watching old movies from the early 20th century, one is struck by how men, of all classes, wore hats. In fact, almost all the hats we wear now were designed and created during the 1920s and 1930s. Men wore hats all year round: Spring and summer brought out lightweight hats like straw boaters, Panamas, and cotton flat caps; fall and winter weather called for heavy felt Fedoras, Homburgs, and Derbies; and for formal occasions a top hat was worn. By the 1960s hat wearing had declined, only to resurface during the 1980s and 1990s, with younger generations wearing baseball caps, Kangols, and bucket hats.

When drawing a hat, remember to draw the hat fitting firmly on the head. The various types of hats might look different, but they should all have a crown that fits securely around the forehead.

Figure 5.41b Hat man 2020. Image courtesy of George Gozum.

Figure 5.41c Image courtesy of Richard Haines.

Figure 5.41a "Yellow Bucket hat" illustration by the author.

Figure 5.42 Top hat illustration by the author.

Diagrams: The Right and Wrong Way a Hat Fits on the Head

Figure 5.43a Remember to draw the hat sitting firmly on the head.

Figure 5.43b Remember to draw the hat sitting firmly on the head.

Cowboy

Homburg

Cowboy (side)

Trapper

Newsboy

Wide-brim Stetson

Figure 5.44 Remember to draw the hat sitting firmly on the head.

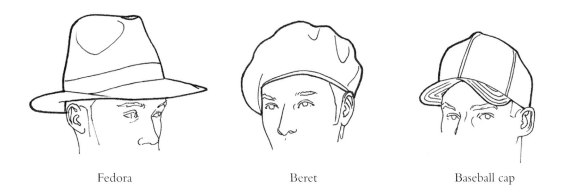

Fedora

Beret

Baseball cap

SHOES

The shoe, in one form or another, has always been with us. Whether as a sandal, a cloth boot, or a wooden clog, shoes have been a necessary item for men and women since the beginning of civilization. The modern men's shoe, with an arched sole and a heel, emerged at the end of the 16th century; over the course of the next two hundred years, these additions slowly became more popular. By the mid-19th century, with the rise of factories, most shoes were mass-produced. Because of the rise in personal incomes and the increasing popularity of sports and other activities, there was a gradual demand for a diverse range of styles.

Since the 1970s, the sneaker, or trainer, has become a ubiquitous footwear choice for men of all ages. This is due to the casualization of menswear, the influence of black street culture, and the marketing of global sportswear companies like Nike and Adidas.

Unless you are a menswear shoe designer, it is doubtful that you will have to focus solely on the drawing of a shoe. Nevertheless, like any other accessory, the right shoe or boot can only add to the success of a design sketch or illustration.

In drawing shoes, remember that the shoe will follow the form and shape of the foot. With a front view, make sure to emphasize the arch containing the shoelaces and tongue of the shoe. With a three-quarter view, depending on which side of the shoe is being shown, pay attention to the space between the heel and the ball of the foot (underneath the arch). See example.

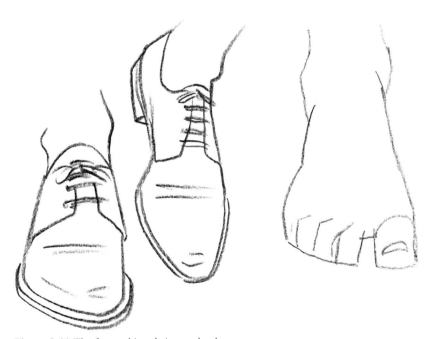

Figure 5.46 The foot and its relation to the shoe.

Figure 5.45 Men's shoes.

ILLUSTRATED GLOSSARY OF SHOE STYLES

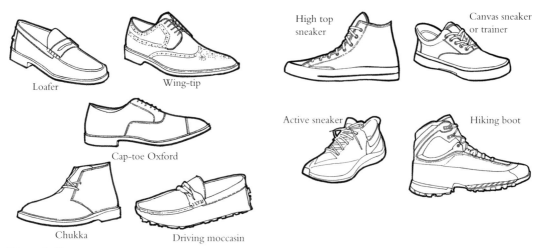

Loafer

Wing-tip

Cap-toe Oxford

Chukka

Driving moccasin

High top sneaker

Canvas sneaker or trainer

Active sneaker

Hiking boot

Figure 5.47

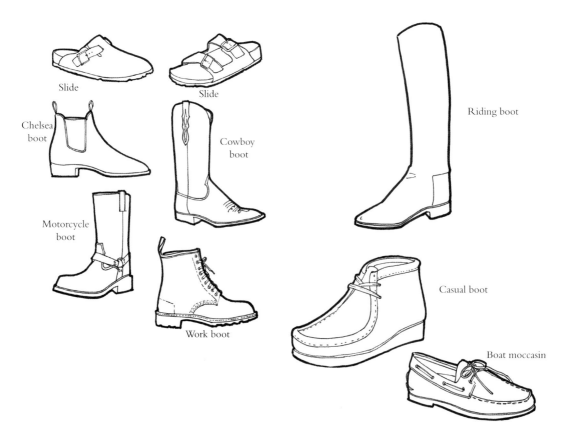

Slide

Slide

Chelsea boot

Cowboy boot

Riding boot

Motorcycle boot

Work boot

Casual boot

Boat moccasin

Figure 5.48 Image courtesy of Gary Kaye. Gary Kaye / view-publications.com.

Figure 5.49 Menswear accessories.

BAGS

When we think of handbags, we typically think of a woman's handbag, but men have worn bags ever since they had things to carry. Before pockets were invented, bags were a staple of menswear. In the Middle Ages men wore a girdle pouch that allowed them to carry everything from herbs and flowers—to mask bodily odors—to food and knives. Most bags were made from leather or wool. During the Renaissance wealthy men wore bags made of jewels and beads and other precious metals. In the 1940s and 1950s the briefcase or attaché case was the choice of lawyers and other businessmen. By the late 20th century, bags had become an essential part of a man's wardrobe. Today the undiminished vogue for men's bags includes, but is not limited to, the backpack, tote, and messenger bag. Like any accessory, it is important that its addition adds to the general theme and look of the fashion figure, unless, of course, the bag is the focal point of the illustration.

ILLUSTRATED GLOSSARY OF BAGS

Briefcase

Backpack

Tote bag

Messenger

Portfolio or Satchel

Leather tote

Figure 5.50 Bag glossary.

ACCESSORIES

Designing accessories, hats, shoes, bags, and eyewear is a specialized field. Each accessory can have different markets and categories. Some accessory designers design for several markets, while others create exclusively for one. The drawing of accessories requires the same levels of observation and draftsmanship that are needed for clothing. A successful accessory designer or illustrator must be an adept draftsman with a good rendering technique, a knowledge of perspective, and an intuitive sense of what makes a good layout. Whether creating sketches during a conceptual phase or for finished illustrations for presentation, studying the construction, proportion, color, and finishing details of an object is unquestionably important.

Recently, some menswear accessories have become almost as important as designer clothing. What was once viewed as an afterthought has now become, for many, an important part of their wardrobe. Tote bags, sneakers, and eyeglasses are now regarded as essential elements of any menswear luxury brand. While such brands have yet to create the all-important investment pieces to rival some women's couture houses, it is only a matter of time before such items are promoted and sold, not just as accessories, but as luxury status items.

Figure 5.51 Image courtesy of Loretta Tedeschi-Cuoco 2020.

Figure 5.52 Image courtesy of Richard Kilroy.

Figure 5.53 Image courtesy of Ryan McMenamy.

6

Rendering Techniques

Color Rendering: Marker, Color Pencils, Watercolor, Gouache, Collage, and Mixed Media

To render a drawing is to embellish it. This is done by adding texture, shading, highlights, and color. Color adds visual complexity to a line drawing by introducing depth and pattern. Color can be descriptive or symbolic—it can even suggest psychological meaning. Color, depending on how it's used and what you are trying to convey, can be even more important than line.

For a fashion designer, or an illustrator, convincingly rendering a fabric in color is an important skill. Being able to accurately describe a particular fabric is just another way of clearly articulating the garment you see or imagine.

That sounds easier than it is. One must carefully observe the distinct characteristics of a fabric, its color, weight, and texture, and then try to mimic those qualities in a drawing. The rendering can be realistic or a mere suggestion, but it must attempt to faithfully communicate the look of the chosen fabric. This is where rendering techniques come in. That does not mean that your rendering must be photographic. In fact, a loose interpretation is often more effective than a strict copy. But your rendering should give a clear-cut idea of what the fabric looks like.

In this chapter we will look at different types of color media, and their use in replicating a wide variety of menswear fabrics. Rendering techniques will vary depending on the media: whether wet, which would include markers, watercolor, inks, and gouache, or dry, which would include color pencils, pastels, and collage, or even a combination of all the above. Your choices will depend on your comfort and ease with a medium, and its suitability for the project you have in mind. An abstract print might be best rendered with markers or gouache, while a

Figure 6.1 Illustration by author.

Figure 6.2 Image courtesy of Renaldo Barnette.

Working with Color

THE BASICS

Remember your first box of crayons? If you do, you might recall mixing your primary colors and creating secondary colors: Red and yellow make orange, yellow and blue make green, and blue and red make purple. When we add these colors together, we get in-between shades, and when we group all these colors together, we have a color wheel. The first color wheel was invented by Sir Isaac Newton in 1672. While studying white light through a prism, he noticed that the light reflected a spectrum of colors, in effect a rainbow. Newton discovered that when white light passes through transparent mediums of different densities, that light is broken down into different wavelengths, or colors. We see color because light waves are reflected from objects into our eyes. Seeing these different hues, Newton compared them to musical notes. He then eventually arranged these notes, or colors, on a rotating disk to see how they would relate to one another. This color wheel was soon expanded to include primary, secondary, and tertiary colors, twelve in all.

Primary colors are red, yellow, and blue. These are source colors, and do not need to be mixed; they are the source of the other colors. **Secondary** colors are orange, green, and violet. These colors are made by mixing two primary colors. **Tertiary** colors are the product of mixing a primary color with a secondary color. They are red-orange, yellow-orange, yellow-green, blue-green, blue-violet, and red-violet. Words like *value*, *tint*, *tone*, and *intensity* are used to describe the appearance of a color. *Value* is the darkness or lightness of a color. Adding black to a color will produce a *shade*; adding white to a color will

complicated print might suggest a photo collage; digital rendering—Adobe Photoshop and Adobe Illustrator—will be covered in the next chapter. Rendering techniques can often differ from one artist to another, and there is always another way to see and render a fabric. However, as with all methods, you must practice and experiment in order to find out what suits you. In other words, you must know the rules before you can bend or break them. Each medium will force an artist to adapt and change, often leading to a new style or approach. This is how an artist or designer grows. Once you have mastered a medium, find a new one. Through practice, you will not only familiarize yourself with a particular medium, but you'll also discover which media you prefer, while refining your own method. A bonus is the discovery of new ways to communicate.

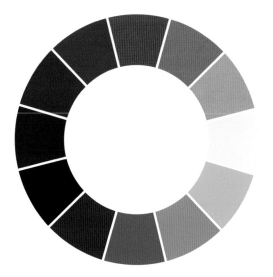

Figure 6.3a Full color wheel.

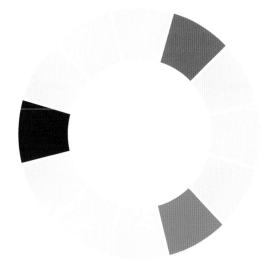

Figure 6.3c Secondary colors.

Figure 6.3b Primary colors.

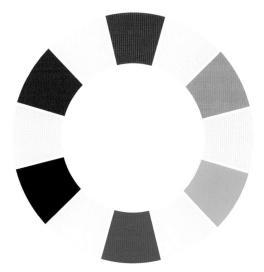

Figure 6.3d Tertiary colors.

produce a *tint*. For example, pink is a tint of red. A *tone* is when gray is added to a color. *Intensity*, not to be confused with value, is the brightness or dullness of color. Warm colors are colors usually associated with warm things: red, yellow, and orange. Cool colors are colors that are usually associated with cool things: blue, purple, green.

COLOR SCHEMES

Colors that work well together are called a color scheme. A **monochromatic** color scheme is the use of colors of the same hue, but in different shades or tints.

An **analogous** scheme is when colors next to one another on the color wheel are used.

Complementary colors are colors that are directly across from one another on the color wheel.

A **split complementary** is a combination of a color plus two colors next to the complement: for example, blue, yellow, and orange.

A **triadic combination** is a color scheme where the colors are evenly spaced around the color wheel. Triadic colors seem to both harmonize and contrast at the same time.

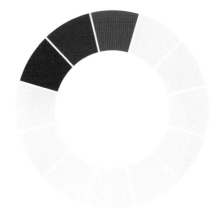

Figure 6.4b Analogous scheme.

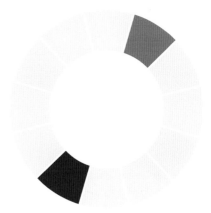

Figure 6.4c Complementary colors.

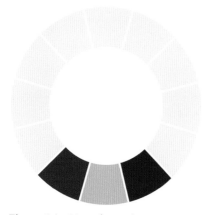

Figure 6.4a Monochromatic.

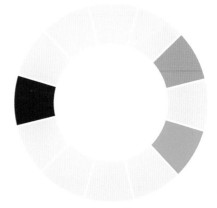

Figure 6.4d Split complementary colors.

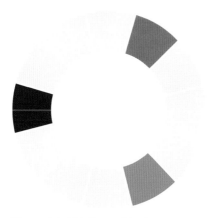

Figure 6.4e Triadic combination.

Wet Media

MARKERS

Markers have been the preferred medium for fashion designers for decades, and it's easy to see why. Markers are quick and easy, and there are a vast array of colors to choose from, making the need to create a particular color almost unnecessary. They can be layered with other markers, blended with marker blenders, or texturized with color pencils. There are two different types of markers: alcohol-based and water-based. Alcohol-based markers contain dye ink and are the choice of most professionals. Because of the dye, there is less likelihood of getting streaks, or lines, in one's art. They typically have a wider range of vibrant colors than water-based markers, dry quickly, and are relatively permanent. The downside is that alcohol-based markers are expensive, can dry up fast, can have an unpleasant smell, and, like most markers, are impossible to correct with erasers or paint.

Water-based markers are odorless due to the lack of solvents and will not bleed through paper as much as alcohol-based markers, but

Figure 6.5

Figure 6.6

too much color or pressure and the paper can warp and damage. They also take longer to dry than alcohol-based markers and are not waterproof. Many markers come in sets, and while that may appear to be economical, buying a set usually means purchasing several colors you will rarely use. It's better to buy markers individually, gradually building a palette that reflects your own taste or current assignment. You can always buy markers of a particular color when needed.

A few general rules:

Marker paper: Unlike regular drawing paper, marker paper is specifically made for markers. It is typically a thin, opaque paper with a smooth coated surface and a treated back that will have little to no bleed when used with alcohol-based markers. It is essential that you try out different marker papers to see which works best with your chosen marker. Different manufacturers will produce different types of paper; only by testing them out with a variety of markers will you be able to see what is right for you. Depending on the amount of layering and blending, a marker paper with a smooth front and a coating on the back might prevent the ink from bleeding through. If your technique involves heavier layering, then a thicker paper like Bristol paper might be a better choice.

Marker brands: Some common brands of alcohol-based marker include Prismacolor, Copic, Chartpak, Tombow, Sakura Koi, Faber-Castell, and Sharpie. The list of water-based markers includes Crayola, Sakura, Staedtler, Tombow, Winsor & Newton, Pentel, and Caran d'Ache. Many markers are double- or even triple-sided, with a small tip on one side, and either a larger chisel tip or a brush on the other side. Each brand of marker is different, with its own set of strengths and weaknesses. Some markers are matched to the Pantone Matching System, making it faster and easier to use than paint. Others, like Copic markers, can be refilled, some straight from the bottle. You might notice warm-gray markers tend to be slightly reddish, while cold-gray markers are slightly bluish. Be sure you test the marker on the paper you intend to use, and then, if possible, check your marker color in color-corrected light.

Thin marker pens such as Sakura Pigma's Micron Pen can be used as holding lines, or as aids in rendering seams, buttons, and other smaller garment details. These fine point pens come in various point sizes and can be bought as a set or individually. Other fine point pens include "gel" pens. Gel pens are water-based and come in white, metallics, and some light colors. Because gel pens are somewhat opaque, these light-colored pens are often used to add texture or detail to dark colors.

Technique

The simplest approach to rendering with markers is to think in terms of layering—of first putting down a flat color, and then adding another layer of color on top of it. While markers are a convenient wet medium, one of their drawbacks is streaking. If you move too fast to cover an area, you will create streaks. Instead of a flat tone, you'll see uneven lines of the white of the paper showing through. You can minimize this effect by using a blender marker—a blender is a colorless alcohol-based marker that is used to disperse or blend a marker color. Keep in mind that a blending marker is unfortunately not for blending two colors together.

You could also lessen the look of streaks by adding another layer of the same color, creating a darker or more saturated shade. Just like a watercolor or an oil painting, or even a digital illustration, building a color by adding layers—with markers or color pencils, with the same or different colors—can intensify (saturate) or strengthen a color (tone or hue), or help develop shadow and light (value). Layered rendering can also create textures, patterns, volume, and dimension. One can render a figure flatly, creating a highly stylized fashion drawing, or work realistically, developing a drawing with depth and weight through shading and highlights. Markers work well for that particular effect. However, these are choices that must play out through experimentation and testing. Marker nibs will dictate what type of stroke you get. Chisel tips, useful for covering large areas, can create thick or thin lines depending on the angle of the nib. Fine-tip nibs are good for filling in details or small areas. Brush-tip markers mimic the thick and thin stroke of a paint brush. In other words, you must use the markers on a paper you plan to use to see what the effect is. Almost all complex renderings require some planning. That's just part of the creative process, but it can also be fun.

Begin by using a 4H or 6H pencil for the underdrawing on marker paper. Sketch lightly. Pencils this hard can be used without the pencil lines showing; if they do, you can erase them later with a kneaded eraser. The first layers should always be the lightest shades. By adding additional layers of color, either with markers or color pencils, you can create more depth and dimension; also, it is always easier go darker in tone, rather than lighter, in a rendering. Start at the top of your drawing and drag the color toward the bottom. When you have finished coloring, add your outlines in either color pencils, using black, or a darker shade of the color used for the

Figure 6.7 Image courtesy of Renaldo Barnette.

garment, or use a fine point black pen. Be sure to add folds and shadows either with a darker color of the clothes, or with a black or dark-gray pencil. Go over areas of garment details, like pockets, seams, and buttons, with a fine point marker (0.1) or a finely sharpened black pencil.

WATERCOLOR AND DYES

There was a time when every fashion designer and illustrator worked with watercolor or gouache. The seemingly endless uses of wet media seemed a perfect way to communicate the ever-changing look of fashion. The unique nature of watercolors and dyes, that distinctive ability to create images through the manipulation of washes, brushstrokes, and layers, has allowed artists to express themselves in a variety of ways for centuries. Before the invention

Figure 6.8 Illustration by author.

and intuitive—there is the look of watercolor: its transparency, vibrancy, dynamism, and elegance. That is because when we talk about watercolor, or inks, we're talking about drawing with water, color, and brush. Though the medium might be intimidating at first, once you become familiar with all its peculiarities and possibilities, you are certain to enjoy its unique effects. Dyes are similar to inks, but these concentrated colors are meant to be diluted with water. The colors of dyes, even combined with water, are dramatic and vivid. Dyes work like watercolor and can be handled in the same way.

A Few Additional Points

You can find the list of art supplies for watercolor in Chapter 2. Even so, there are still a few other things to remember: Like some other media, watercolor can be divided into two style types: one tight and realistic, the other loose and spontaneous. A tight rendering will need precision and planning, typically with an underdrawing. Areas will need to be marked or perhaps masked, and attention to detail—shadows and highlights—along with garment details, will require focus. A loose rendering, on the other hand, will need equal parts spontaneity and confidence. There may or may not be an underdrawing. The brush marks you make must be precise, but also impressionistic. And then, having said all of that, one must also allow for the unexpected or happy "mistake"; that is, an accident that can somehow greatly add to a drawing. With wet media this is bound to happen, even with some planning, because watercolor is so unpredictable. That is both its virtue and its weakness.

Figure 6.9 Watercolor illustration by author.

of markers in the 1950s, paint was not only the traditional method of fashion drawing; it was also the only method. However, since markers and digital programs have become more widely used, watercolor has become less popular. While markers have an attractive immediacy, watercolor takes time: One must often mix colors and consider the effect. It can also be a mercurial and unforgiving medium: Mistakes are hard to correct, and it requires a certain level of skill.

Nevertheless, watercolor still has much to recommend it. Aside from the unique kinesthetic experience of painting—the feel of a wet brush gliding against the paper, at once exacting

Figure 6.10 Image courtesy of Richard Vyse.

Figure 6.11 Image courtesy of Richard Vyse.

Regardless of your approach, don't be timid. As for brushes, different brushes will produce different effects. A smaller, tapered brush, say a #0, will cover smaller areas like the face or hands, but will also work well when painting garment details. A similarly tapered #4 watercolor brush can easily cover a ten-inch fashion figure. A larger, wide, and flat brush is great for covering larger areas on much bigger drawings. Note that we're discussing watercolor brushes, not oil or acrylic brushes. The successful use of any brush with a wet medium requires constant practice and experimentation. Achieving a professional look depends on mastering not only the materials but, perhaps more importantly, the technique. One such important technique is "the wash."

Figure 6.12 Illustration by author.

Figure 6.13a R&B Hermann: Images courtesy of Fashion Institute of Technology SUNY FIT Library of Special Collections and College Archives.

Figure 6.13b R&B Hermann: Images courtesy of Fashion Institute of Technology SUNY FIT Library of Special Collections and College Archives.

Technique

For fashion illustrators in the recent past, the term "wash drawing" was used to describe a sketch done in tones of gray. These drawings were then reproduced in halftones for newspaper advertisements. But, broadly speaking, a wash is a simple watercolor technique that consists of loading your brush with a wet color and applying it evenly on paper, thereby creating a flat, unmarked, painted area. It is a technique that is not particularly hard to learn but does take some practice. For tonal variations it's important to remember that the intensity of a wash depends on the amount of water added to the color. More water will dilute the color, making it lighter and transparent, and less water will darken the color, making it opaque. Superimposing several washes will create darker tones.

Since watercolor dries quickly, it is best to have everything at the ready. Be sure to have all your material carefully set up before you begin. It is always a good idea to work on a slanted surface, either an adjustable drawing table or a slanted drawing board, alongside a flat surface for water jars, paint, palette, and paper towels. Paper towels or clean rags will be needed to blot excess paint and water. As discussed in Chapter 2 on art supplies, watercolor paper varies in thickness, texture, and price, but in the beginning an inexpensive 140 lb. cold-press paper should do. Avoid paper with too rough a surface unless you plan to work at a large scale.

Figure 6.14 How to apply a wash.

HOW TO APPLY A WASH

1. Begin by drawing a variety of shapes (circles, squares, triangles—large and small) on a sheet of watercolor paper. These are the shapes you will use for practice.

2. Using a tube of watercolor—preferably a darker color—squeeze a small amount onto a palette and dilute it with water. Make enough to fill in all the shapes. Make tests on a separate piece of paper. (This minor point is very important: Testing the look of your watercolor before applying it, making sure it is neither too opaque nor too weak, is vital.) Be sure to have your paper towel or rag close by for blotting your brushes.

3. Make sure your work is on a slanted surface: It is because of the tilted surface that the excess watercolor can be pulled down by gravity and the brush, thus avoiding puddles and streaks. Using plenty of watercolor on your brush, start with a brushstroke at the top of your shape from the left-hand area. Then move the brush across the top of the shape, all while pulling the excess water, or wash, to the right. Imagine you are quickly reading a text from left to right with the point of your brush, and then back again. This must be done quickly. If you are too slow, the paint in the wash will settle, creating lines once the wash is dry. Dip the brush in your color again and apply the next stroke, dragging the first and puddling it, overlapping the color each time. Never let your brush go dry, and never go over an area that has already been painted. Work as quickly and evenly as you can until you reach the bottom. At the bottom you may have a puddle. Quickly blot your brush dry, then, using the tip, sop up the excess puddle.

    As the area dries, the wash should be a flat, even tone. It is also possible to repeat the process if you want a deeper tone, but that means working with a thinner wash to avoid streaking, and only once the work is completely dry. Since a wash can't be corrected—and any attempt to do so will only further damage the piece—it is best to work quickly and methodically. Once you get the hang of it, the technique will become second nature. With more experience, one can create subtle shadows, either with a wet-on-wet approach or by adding another tone once the area is dry. Practice and experimentation are key here. As you work, you will discover how best to control the medium before going on to a finished drawing.

4. There are several different watercolor techniques with which you can experiment, and most have to do with brushstrokes. There is the wet-on-wet technique, which produces a soft blurry effect. Begin with either a still-damp wash or a wet paper. Start by simply making marks with your paintbrush. You will notice the brushstrokes expand and feather. This technique is useful for suggesting soft textures like chiffon, or even fur. There is the dry brush approach. That is when one applies a semi-dry, or barely moist, brush on a wet or dry area. This will produce tiny brushstrokes that can be used to describe textures as different as hair or shadows.

When using watercolor for figure drawing, one can, with some skill, create numerous textures and effects (those fabric textures and effects will be discussed later in this chapter). But perhaps the simplest way to use watercolor for a fashion figure is to paint a wash for different parts of a clothed figure. For example, in painting a jacket one might paint a wash on a jacket arm, then paint the opposite arm, then the left side of the jacket, then the right. In this way one could wait for a section to dry while working on another area, without worrying about the two adjacent areas bleeding into one another. Another tip is to always end the wash where natural seams and ends of a garment would occur, thus giving your drawing a seamless look. Also, by adding another layer of wash over a dry wash, you can produce a darker or more intense wash. And by adding a darker tone of your wash to your figure, you can suggest shadows or texture. More complicated tonal effects can be achieved by drawing a wet brush against the edge of a still-damp wash edge. This will dissolve and blur what was a hard line.

5. After you have finished, you may want to clean your illustration of pencil lines. Wait until the painting is completely dry before applying a kneaded eraser over those lines you wish to remove.

RENDERING PLAIN WEAVE FABRIC

A plain, or flat, weave is a woven fabric with vertical warp threads and horizontal weft threads that create a larger whole. It is the simplest and most common of the three basic weaves (the other two being twill and satin). The look of plain weave can vary depending on the thickness, texture, and color of the yarn. It has no pile, hence the word "flat," but the fabric may have some uneven coarseness due to the size of the yarns. A wool sportscoat (wool being the most common fabric for men's suits) would be rendered as a flat color with details and shadows, but with few or no highlights, because wool tends to absorb light.

TEXTURED FABRICS RENDERED IN COLOR: MARKERS AND WATERCOLORS

Textured fabrics are typically opaque, which makes them easier to illustrate. When rendering such fabrics—like tweed, wool flannel, camel hair, and gabardine—start with a base color, then focus on the fabric's look and texture by adding mid-tones and shadows. Keep highlights to a minimum.

Figure 6.15 Step-by-step watercolor rendering—blue trench coat.

GOUACHE

As mentioned in Chapter 2, Gouache (pronounced *gwash*) is a type of water media. The biggest difference between watercolor and gouache is that watercolor is translucent, and gouache is opaque. Many artists have used gouache because of its heavier and denser qualities. It works best in either flat poster art or gestural and direct paintings. However, gouache can also be watered down and used with an almost transparent watercolor effect. Both paints consist of pigment and a water-soluble binder, but the opacity of gouache comes from the white pigment or chalk that is added. When a layer of watercolor is applied over a drawing, the light can travel through the paint layer and reflect off the white of the paper, giving the painting a luminous transparency. A gouache painting has a flat matte finish that leaves none of the paper showing.

Today, gouache isn't quite as popular as other styles of paint, though that wasn't always the case: For many commercial artists in the past, it was a quick alternative to oil or watercolor. It was, and still is, an adaptable paint, easy to apply with brush, pen, or airbrush. Now its main fault seems to be that, like all wet media, it can be time consuming. But it still has its virtues. Gouache dries quickly and darker than watercolor, it mixes well with other colors, and can be heavily applied without noticeable brushstrokes.

To lighten a color, one simply adds white. Gouache is also very forgiving, mistakes made can be easily covered up, and it works well with art that requires precision. Some gouache paintings can even rival digital art in their clarity and brightness. With its relatively quick ease of use, its flat matte finish, and its ability to reproduce well, it remains a favorite among many illustrators.

A Few Additional Points

One can find gouache in almost any art supply store. The paint can be found in tubes, such as in designer series, or in jars of poster paint. Most artists plan their illustrations with a pencil underdrawing, using a heavy watercolor paper or illustration board. Usually, they mask areas where lines or paint are not wanted with frisket film, an adhesive paper, or masking tape. (Note: Masking or painter's tape is a type of pressure-sensitive tape made with an easily released adhesive. Like frisket, it is used to mask off borders or areas that should not be painted. Art masking fluid is similar to frisket but is a liquid-latex-based product that is used to keep small areas of a watercolor unpainted. The rubber prevents the paint from reaching the paper and is peeled off with a rubber cement pickup. At a pinch, you can use rubber cement as a masking fluid. Just allow it to dry and paint over it.) The flat painted areas can be subtly modeled with darker and lighter applications of the same color, creating texture and dimension. As mentioned earlier, while gouache is very forgiving, experimentation and practice is strongly suggested.

Figure 6.16 Antonio. Missoni Spring Summer 1985 campaign, model unknown. Acrylic on paper. The Estate & Archives of Antonio Lopez and Juan Ramos.

Figure 6.17 Gouache rendering. Illustration by author.

Color Pencils

Few designers, or illustrators, use color pencils exclusively. A large, finished pencil drawing simply takes too long to finish. However, they are an intriguing medium capable of creating beautiful effects, particularly when combined successfully with pens or markers. The characteristics of color pencils combine the fluid line of a graphite pencil with the tonal variations and color of watercolor. Besides linear drawing, there is the ability to create different effects with the overlay of two or more colors. In short, there is more to color pencils than one might assume.

There are two types of color pencils: wax-based and oil-based. The wax-based pencil is the one most often used. They cover a wide range of grades, from softcore pencils to hard-leaded sticks. They also come in a wealth of colors, and in all shapes and sizes. Wax-based color pencils are more durable, given their harder cores, and are less expensive than oil-based pencils. Oil-based color pencils are messier, as their description might suggest. While the effect

Figure 6.18 Red man. Illustration by author.

Figure 6.19 Marker and color pencil design illustrations by the author.

is often beautiful, it might be considered too troublesome for a fashion sketch, because despite the apparent hardness of the core, the application will smear. On the plus side, an oil-based color pencil will quickly dispense color over an area, so additional layering is not required. But because they use up more color, they are less durable and more expensive. Using oil-based color pencils is something of a specialized skill, so they are typically used by artists who are well versed in the medium. Still, it is an option.

As with all media, there are a range of products available of varying levels of quality. For a beginner, cheaper, student-grade materials should suffice, but if you can afford the higher-grade pencils, you'll certainly notice the difference. The best color pencils will move effortlessly across the paper instead of dragging, and their colors will also have a noticeable richness and vibrancy. They'll also blend more easily. That is a quality that is useful when paired with markers. Generally, when color pencil is applied over a marker base, it is to alter the color or texture of the area, which involves several techniques. Another type of color pencil is water-soluble; these can be used for a traditional watercolor effect. Apply the water-soluble pencil as you would any color pencil. Then, with a watercolor brush, add a layer of water. This will activate the color, covering the white of the paper.

Figure 6.20 Antonio, "Follow the Leaders," *GHQ Magazine*, James Dean 1977. The Estate & Archives of Antonio Lopez and Juan Ramos.

Messrs. America

The style of clean jeans and a great plaid shirt, what could be more American! That's how sportswear began, and now after traveling the world, they're back together again as the up-country, down home way of living becomes the role to dress. That's why the plaids are plain and simple and unsubtle. In a word, colorful. As for jeans, though the frills are gone, this means the details count more than ever before.

Left to right: Cotton plaid shirt, and a cotton elastic back jeans from Brittania;
Geno cotton and rayon plaid with A. Smile cotton corduroy jeans and lambskin vest from Remy;
Levi's tartan plaid shirt in polyester/cotton, and Levi's cotton jeans with corduroy trim;
Joel plaid, in triacetate and polyester, with cotton jeans from Hang Ten Slacks and Jeans.

BRITTANIA

GENO
A. SMILE
REMY

LEVI'S

JOEL
HANG TEN
SLACKS and JEANS

illustration by Robert Melendez 3/15/1976

Figure 6.21 DNR San Diego 1976: Image courtesy of Robert Melendez.

TECHNIQUE

The basic techniques of color pencil involve a combination of shading and line. By using the effects of light and shadow, one can add elements of realism to a drawing, suggesting depth and form. Since we're starting with a line drawing and then adding a flat layer of color with marker, developing a tonal range with various tones and hues not only helps to describe the garment, but also gives weight and volume to the figure itself. Stark contrasts of light and shadow seldom work with fashion design drawings—they're too dramatic. Instead, a gradual progression from light to dark, with in-between shadings and highlights, is more realistic.

To start, there is the basic back and forth, a way of rendering so elementary, it's almost instinctive. Simply move the pencil back and forth until you gradually build a shadow or until you cover the intended area. A pencil color the same color as the marker, but with perhaps a darker hue, will build depth. By adding a color pencil of an even darker color, say black, will further deepen the shadows and add more contrast. This is perhaps the most common use of color pencils among fashion designers: for the slow building of shadows and highlights. It is important to remember that the pressure you apply while drawing will determine the brightness and density of your color. As a rule, the lighter the pressure, the lighter the application of color. It is also easier to add dark colors over light colors, than light colors over dark, though white pencils are often the exception to the rule.

Hatching: This technique involves making straight parallel lines next to one another. Gradually, as the lines get closer together and the pressure increases, the area becomes darker. The lines can be diagonal, vertical, or horizontal, just as long as they don't touch.

Crosshatching: This involves crossing the parallel lines in hatching, which go in one direction, with parallel lines in another direction.

Layering: This is when two colors blend to become a third color. Layering isn't a technique that is used very often among designers, because it is time consuming and requires some skill. But the effect can be impressive.

Burnishing: This technique involves applying heavy pressure with a color pencil, flattening the texture of the paper, and filling the space completely. Some artists use a blending stump, some use the pencil, but the end effect should be a polished, glazed look.

Whitening: This is the technique of blending the colors of your drawing with a white pencil. It has the effect of polishing, lightening, and mixing the surface colors. This process will also give your drawing a glossy creamy finish.

Blending with a marker blender: By applying a marker blender to a penciled surface, you can smooth out the pigment and give the area a darker and more matte finish.

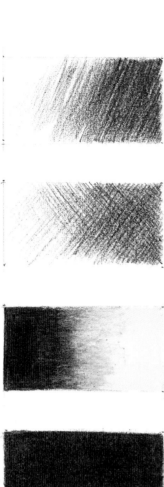

Figure 6.22a Hatching.

Figure 6.22b Crosshatching.

Figure 6.22c Layering.

Figure 6.22d Burnishing.

Figure 6.22e Whitening.

Figure 6.22f Blending with a marker blender on a color pencil surface.

Pastels

Pastels are similar in appearance and consistency to chalk, but softer and slightly more opaque. Artist's chalks are generally limited to white, black, sepia, brown, and sanguine (red-brown), while pastels have a much wider color palette. Pastels are rarely used in fashion art, because they don't lend themselves to detail work, and for the newcomer they can be time consuming, unpredictable, and messy. Nevertheless, for editorial fashion art, pastels can be very effective. There is a chromatic richness, texture, and boldness that is very attractive. As mentioned in Chapter 2, there are two types of pastels: soft and oil. Soft pastels have a smooth, velvety texture that allows bits of the paper underneath to show through. Oil pastels leave a greasy smudge that can be worked on, usually with water or a turpentine dilution. This technique is a favorite among artists who favor a more abstract and painterly representation of the figure. Given that oil pastels cannot be blended by rubbing, a turpentine dilution is a convenient alternative for mixing color. Keep in mind that whatever pastel you decide to use, your choice of paper—medium-grained or rough—is bound to affect the final look of your drawing.

Figure 6.23 Image courtesy of Leonard Cadiente. @bycadiente.

Collage and Mixed Media

Collage, from the French word *coller*, meaning "to glue" or "to stick," is an art technique involving the assemblage of different images and forms to create new art. Collage, or mixed media, often uses magazine or newspaper clippings, along with bits of fabric, photographs, color paper, sometimes even printed texts and found objects. Though an old technique, it wasn't until the early 20th century, through the work of Pablo Picasso and Georges Braque, that the art form became popular. While collage has most often been created by hand, it is now being widely used by fashion artists and designers through digital programs like Photoshop and Illustrator.

Collage can be a dramatic way of creating fashion art. Because handmade collages require cutting and pasting, thereby creating work that is almost three-dimensional, there can be a high level of involvement. Combining textural forms with abstraction, collage, and mixed media allows one to create art that is outside of the usual conventions of fashion art. This is especially true for editorial art, where the idea of the garment is more important than an exact representation.

Begin with a pencil sketch of a clothed figure, then start cutting out forms with colored paper, magazines, or fabrics. The shapes you cut out should exaggerate and yet somehow mimic the silhouette of the figure. Think in terms of contrasts: light and dark, rough and smooth, symmetry and asymmetry, and, above all, composition. Constantly move the shapes around until they coalesce into a dynamic image. Instinct and chance may play a part here, and that is a good thing. Play with the elements. Once you think they work, glue the parts in place. As long as the art conveys some information about the garment, how it looks, and how it's worn, mixed media can be a successful alternative to drawing.

Menswear Fabrics: Rendering Yarn-Dyed Fabrics

Whenever we think of menswear patterned fabrics, we generally think of yarn-dyed fabrics, even if we don't realize it. Checks, stripes, pinstripes, and plaids—these are all yarn-dyed fabrics. Yarn-dyed fabrics are exactly what they sound like: fabrics that are dyed and then woven into a cloth. The surface pattern is literally part of the fabric. To render yarn-dyed woven fabrics, it is best to start with a grid. These patterns, like checks, plaids, tweeds, and herringbones, should be planned, typically with a grid. The goal should be to simplify a pattern as much as possible, and to render the scale of the pattern accurately. Keep in mind that there are many ways to render fabrics. Techniques will vary depending on the media and the fabric being rendered.

DEVELOPING A SWATCH LIBRARY

Before you attempt to render a fabric, it is important that you have a sizable swatch to study and work from. Keep in mind that your swatch, depending upon the pattern, will almost certainly have to be scaled down. To that end, it might be helpful to have either an actual garment with

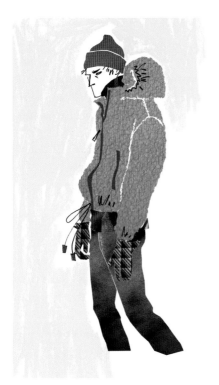

Figure 6.25 Image courtesy of Geoffry Gertz. geoffrygertz.com.

Figure 6.24 Image courtesy of Gary Kaye. Gary Kaye / view-publications.com.

Figure 6.26 Image courtesy of Gary Kaye. Gary Kaye / view-publications.com.

Figure 6.27 Pink suit.

a similarly scaled pattern or a photograph of a garment with the pattern. The best approach is to try and copy a real fabric swatch as closely as possible. Start by rendering the fabric to the same scale as the swatch. Once you've replicated the fabric, it should be easier to render the fabric at a smaller scale. Recreating the fabric in a reduced scale may require simplifying it, but that's not necessarily a bad thing. Your aim should be a straightforward reinterpretation, rather than a photographic copy.

Most fabric stores have policies and set aside times for purchasing fabric swatches, and there are, of course, online resources that might prove useful when searching for vintage fabric swatches, but research is key. You might also invest in a fabric swatch library. Like the reference or swipe file mentioned in Chapter 2, a swatch library can be a convenient and reliable resource. Categorize your fabrics by patterns, weights, or any other type. Filed and notated, your curated fabric library will make it easy for you to pick and choose a particular fabric whenever needed.

Pattern and Texture

RENDERING SIMPLE WOOL PATTERNS

Almost all simple two-color patterns—gingham check, pinstripe, houndstooth, herringbone, and Glen plaid—can, and perhaps should, be created with a grid. Start by placing a sheet of tracing paper over the figure and area you plan to render. Analyze the pattern and its scale before you create the grid. Carefully draw the grid lightly in pencil. Once you are confident of your grid,

retrace the grid onto the marker paper and your intended finished figure. There are three ways to interpret a surface pattern: Draw the pattern following the curve of the body (this is the more realistic approach); draw the pattern flatly, with the straight lines letting the outer lines define the form; or only partially draw the pattern on the garment, letting it fade off into the white of the paper. If done correctly, this effect should look like there is extreme sunlight on one side of the figure.

Assignment: Practice rendering the patterns described.

Materials:

– Tracing paper

– Marker paper

– Gray marker: #5 or 40%, dual point (for the planning stage on tracing paper). For the finish, use whatever colors are part of your design or existing garment.

– Black color pencil and additional color pencils for shading and texture.

Begin by copying any of the patterns in the fabric swatch boxes, then scale them down and place them on a figure. Your initial figure should be one with a simple, easy-to-understand pose. Feel free to change the colors but not the grid pattern. Remember: Before rendering any pattern on a figure, make sure you plan how the pattern will look in terms of its scale and position. Different parts of the garment may require a different positioning of the pattern; for example, the collar, lapels, and pockets. Plan your grid on tracing paper, tracing out the figure. When you are sure of the proportions and scale of the pattern, retrace the figure and the grid on marker paper. In finishing the drawing, use markers for the overall color palette, and pencils and gel pens for fine lines and details.

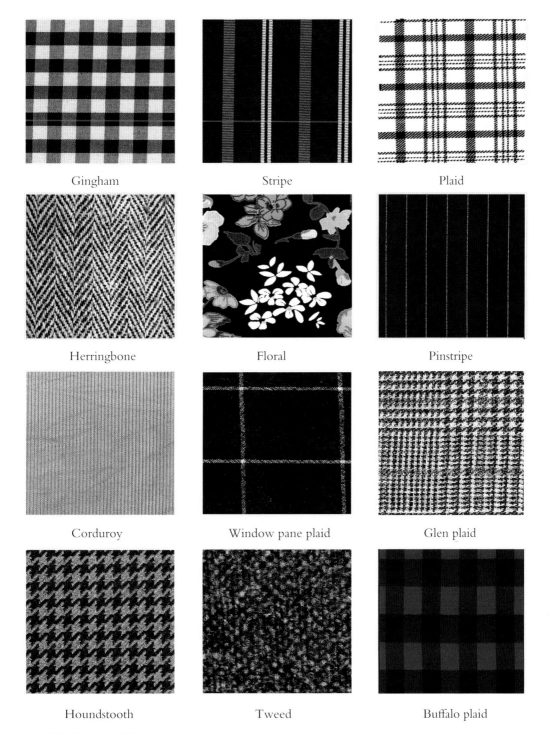

Gingham	Stripe	Plaid
Herringbone	Floral	Pinstripe
Corduroy	Window pane plaid	Glen plaid
Houndstooth	Tweed	Buffalo plaid

Figure 6.28 Glossary of fabric swatches.

Figure 6.29 Figures wearing pinstripe and houndstooth fabrics.

Figure 6.30 Figures wearing pinstripe and houndstooth fabrics.

Figure 6.31 Creating a plaid figure step by step.

Figure 6.32 Three fabric renderings in marker and color pencil.

Figure 6.33 Rendering fabrics: navy jacket and yellow pinstripe pant.

Figure 6.34 Rendering fabrics: pink jacket with black floral T-shirt and white pants.

Figure 6.35 Rendering fabrics: lime green coat over pink and white shirt with yellow print shorts.

Figure 6.36 Rendering fur.

Figure 6.38 Rendering fur.

Figure 6.37 Image courtesy of Tyler Bubb. Figures by Tyler Bubb, 2021.

RENDERING FUR

There are, of course, many different types of fur: chinchilla, shearling, fox, sable, and minx. There are also faux, or fake, furs. But most fur, apart from short-hair furs like Persian lamb or leopard, have volume and size. When we think of luxurious furs, we think of big, plush, exaggerated shapes. And that is what we should aim for when illustrating furs. Begin with a pencil drawing that emphasizes size. Look for the shadows and highlights. In mink, or sable, you will notice a denser shade in the center of the pelt, with the color becoming lighter as the fur thins out. Notice, too, the direction of the hairs on the fur. The combined light and dark, along with the length and direction of the hairs, will supply you with all the information you need. Once you've added the basic color and shadow, add pencil lines, black, white, and any other colors you see, indicating the hair.

Figure 6.39 Rendering animal print.

PLAIDS, STRIPES, AND CHECKS

The aim in illustrating a fabric is often to capture the look of a particular pattern. However, while there is always more than one way to render a fabric, in the beginning it is probably best to begin with a simple and tried-and-true method. Once you become more familiar with the materials and the general approach to rendering, you may find other ways of achieving the similar effects.

Stripes are simply repeated lines that create a graphic whole. Stripes can be thick or thin, and the look of stripes can be affected by both the fabrication and the cut of the garment. For example, woven stripes on a man's button-down shirt will be crisper and appear more uniform than stripes on a jersey cotton long-sleeved T-shirt. Always make sure that the stripes are equidistant from one another and that the stripes are of a uniform thickness. Creating an underdrawing of a grid will ensure uniformity.

Plaids, gingham, and checks are like stripes, except that the stripes now travel vertically and horizontally. Each of these fabric patterns are based on straight lines. Take a close look at your fabric, then start by creating a grid. Remember to size your patterns to fit the scale of the body you've drawn. Decide if your pattern will follow the contours of the body, or if you plan to render the pattern as a flat shape within the figure. If you decide to create a flat pattern, remember to use shading to add depth and form. Begin by drawing either the top-to-bottom stripe or the left-to-right stripe. Once you've finished stripes in one direction, then draw them in the opposite direction carefully observing the distance of the lines from one another. Follow up with a base color and then carefully build the plaid with weft and warp color stripes and boxes. Intersecting thinner lines in darker or lighter colors can be added with color pencils, thin lines of gouache, or opaque gel pens.

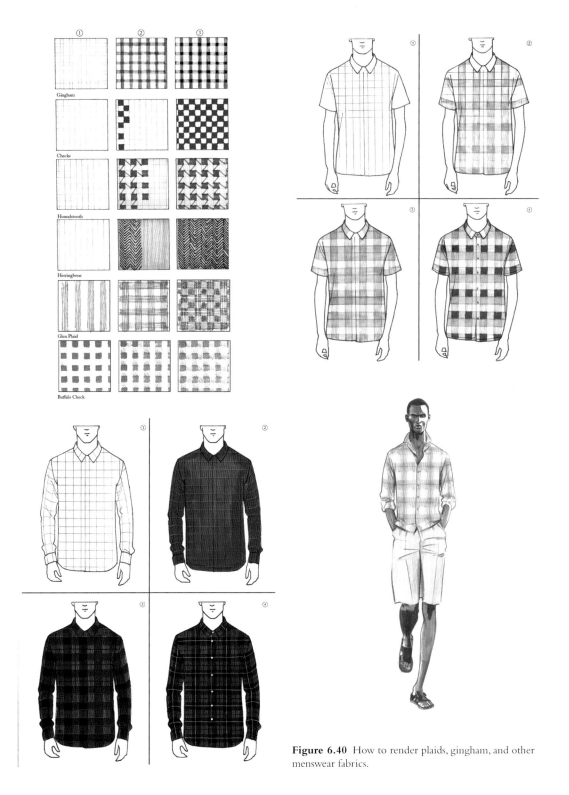

Figure 6.40 How to render plaids, gingham, and other menswear fabrics.

Figure 6.41 How to render a windowpane fabric.

RENDERING FLESH TONES

There are probably a million different skin tones in the world, so the first thing one must decide is which flesh tone looks good with the colors you've chosen for your design or illustration. Other than the choices based on the wishes of a client or personal preference, there is also the purely graphic choice. That is when you choose a skin tone that highlights the color palette of a particular garment or design concept. For example, a white or light color garment might be shown to its best advantage by pairing it with a darker skin tone, and a darker garment might have the requisite graphic punch when using a model with a lighter skin tone. Whether working with markers or watercolor, be sure to test your choices beforehand. You might create a page of skin tones with the marker color name and brand so that you can quickly and easily choose the color you want. Or alternatively, you can premix watercolor versions of skin tones and label them.

Copic marker skin tones

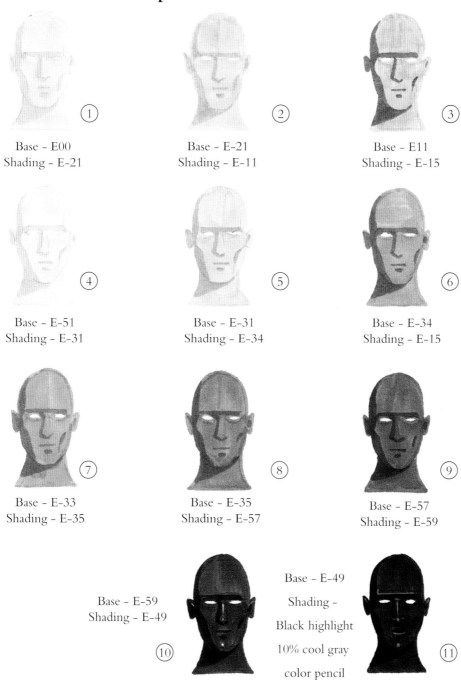

Base – E00
Shading – E-21
①

Base – E-21
Shading – E-11
②

Base – E11
Shading – E-15
③

Base – E-51
Shading – E-31
④

Base – E-31
Shading – E-34
⑤

Base – E-34
Shading – E-15
⑥

Base – E-33
Shading – E-35
⑦

Base – E-35
Shading – E-57
⑧

Base – E-57
Shading – E-59
⑨

Base – E-59
Shading – E-49
⑩

Base – E-49
Shading –
Black highlight
10% cool gray
color pencil
⑪

Figure 6.42 Marker combinations for skintones.

ALL-BLACK RENDERING

There are several ways to render black: One can simply apply the color as a solid, or, to add more tonal values, one can add a layer of black over a dark-gray area. In a stylized rendering, an all-black drawing with white lines indicating seams and garment details can be striking, but for garment renderings requiring shadow and highlights, layers of gray using black as an overlay will create the best effect.

Three images: one in marker and watercolor wash and the third in color pencil.

Figure 6.43b Rendering black fabric in color pencil. Image courtesy of Francisco J. Cortés.

Figure 6.43a Rendering in black marker and watercolor.

Sheer and Shiny Fabrics

RENDERING SHEER FABRICS

Sheer fabrics like chiffon, lace, and various meshes have traditionally been worn by women, but times have changed. Many menswear designers are less hesitant to embrace such formerly gender-specific material in their designs and are willing to explore less conventional ideas of gender. Markers and color pencils can easily imitate the transparency of such fabrics. As in rendering with other media, layering is important. Parts of the body should be visible beneath the fabric, and there will probably be several different values of color depending on the number of sheer layers against the skin. The final look should be soft and airy, with thin lines suggesting fragility and transparency.

① Start with the shape of the skin tone of the body. Leave some white of the paper for highlights and contrasts.

③ Add a holding line in pen. Add additional shadows and folds in a black color pencil.

BLACK LACE

② Add a light gray tone in the shape of the garment. Where there are shadows and folds, use a darker tone of gray.

For netting use crosshatching, add black roses as as an embroidered motif.

Lace fabric with a mesh netting and an embroidered rose motif.

Figure 6.44 Rendering transparent fabrics.

Figure 6.45 Rendering transparent fabrics.

LEATHER AND OTHER SHINY FABRICS

As discussed previously in Chapter 4, shadows and highlights will look different depending on the texture, flexibility, and weight of the fabric. There is a marked difference between the shine of leather and the shine of satin. Something shines when an object, or in this case a fabric, reflects light. Fabrics with a "hard" surface like patent leather or embellishments like sequins and beads, have highly reflective surfaces. Fabrics with a "soft" surface, like velvet, absorb light, creating more subtle highlights and mid-tones. Rendering shine on a figure means being aware of those areas of the garment closest to the light source. In a leg thrust forward as in a *contrapposto* pose, for instance, the planes of the upper thigh would catch the light, while the rear supportive leg would be in relative shadow. Shadows would be created in the recesses of the folds below the knee, with light hitting the tops of those folds. As always, observation is key. Using live models or photographs to study and analyze the various types of shiny fabrics can only help one replicate the effects in a fashion drawing.

Figure 6.46 Walking figure in red hat and black leather jacket.

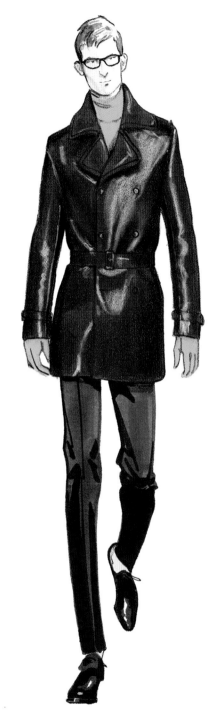

Figure 6.47 Rendering a leather jacket, step by step.

Figure 6.48 Rendering a nylon puffer jacket.

Figure 6.49 Rendering sequin pants.

Repeat Patterns

A repeat pattern is just as described: It is a pattern with a motif that is repeated either vertically, horizontally, or randomly, without a break in design. Typically, a motif (a single element or group of elements) is created as a "tile" of artwork that is then duplicated again and again. The different types of repeats are **one-way**, **two-way**, **half-drop vertical**, **half-drop horizontal**, and **tossed**. (Be aware that every pattern has its own unique look and size; scale and proportion are key.) In order to render a pattern convincingly, you must closely observe and reduce the size of the pattern so that it fits the size of your figure or flat. You can do this by photographing the patterned garment on a model and using it as an accurate measure of scale, or by finding a similar pattern on a figure in a photograph and using that as a guide. A successful rendering of a print is one where the print is recognizable, readable, and in proportion. Remember: Your rendering is an interpretation of the print, not an exact copy. When drawing a pattern manually, either on a figure or a flat, it is best to begin with a grid. Alternatively, many designers create their repeats digitally by using the Offset filter in Photoshop, or the Pattern Options Panel in Illustrator, and incorporate the digital pattern repeats into their illustration accordingly.

Technical Drawings: Flats and Floats

A **flat** is an exact black-and-white technical drawing of a garment as if it were laid out flat on a table. A flat sketch is essentially a blueprint of a garment. These rigorously accurate drawings are usually used to create tech packs. (Note: Tech packs are what they sound like: packets that contain all the technical components and instructions needed by a manufacturer to finish a garment—fabric, grading, seams, colorways, measurements, trims, labels, etc.—and are given to technical designers or patternmakers. They are also used by buyers, salespeople, and production teams, so they must be as specific and readable as possible.) There are different ways to draw a flat; however, the thing to remember is that the flat is less a figurative drawing than a precisely detailed plan for a garment, so silhouette, construction details, fabric indication, and proportion are important. Instead of using a nine-head fashion figure, the figure template for a flat would be closer to an eight-head figure. Flats should include all design details: seams, topstitching, pockets, buttons, and buttonholes, and additional features like pleats or darts. Back views should also be included for a better understanding of the garment.

A **float** is a more stylized version of a flat. The garment drawing will appear more three-dimensional because its proportions are more like a fashion figure, but without an actual body. While they are often used in portfolios and presentations, they are never used in tech packs. There is also a kind of hybrid "**floating flat**." These drawings are not quite as stylized as floats and not as rigid as flats. These sketches have a more expressive fit and silhouette in their appearance; they may have shadows and movement lines, and they are often colored. These types of drawings have become popular because they are easy to visualize and understand, and as such they are used by buyers, salespeople, and merchandisers.

Stripe

Abstract geometric

Geometric

Chintz

Paisley

Conversational

Hawaiian

Ditsy floral

Medium-scale floral

Large-scale floral

Cheetah

Foulard

Figure 6.50 Repeat patterns.

One way

Two way

REPEATS

Half-drop
shift

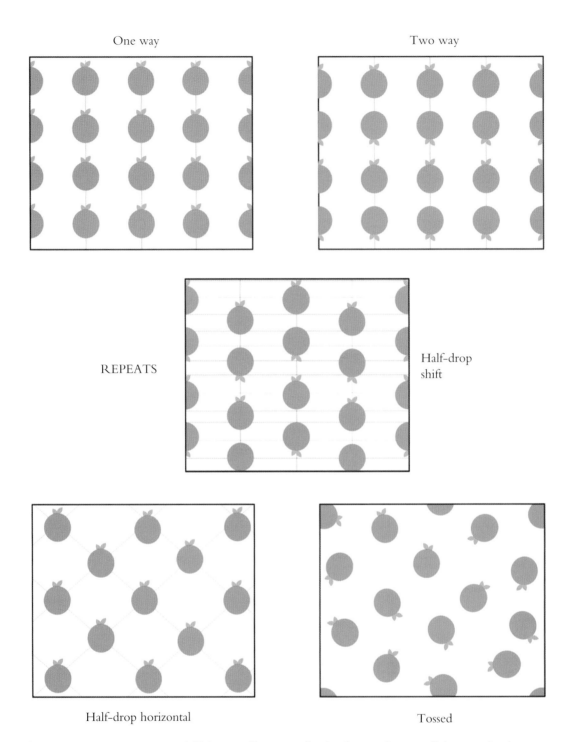

Half-drop horizontal

Tossed

Figure 6.51 Repeat patterns. Apparel fabrics generally use non-directional repeats for more efficient use of yardage.

Figure 6.52 Repeat patterns.

Figure 6.53 Repeat patterns.   **Figure 6.54** Repeat patterns.

HOW TO DRAW A FLAT

Though flats can be drawn digitally—to be covered in the next chapter—it is best to begin practicing this technique by hand to best familiarize yourself with the concept of translating a three-dimensional garment into a two-dimensional drawing. Begin by using your template as a guide, trace your garment on the template body (you can use an existing figure, but it is often best to use your own). Be sure to use the same template for all your flats for scale and consistency. Starting with a larger drawing will allow you to reduce the finished flat to the required size. The drawing will then tighten up, with garment detailing appearing clearer and more precise. Carefully draw half the garment in pencil, then fold over the drawing and trace the other half. This will give your flat a straightforward symmetry. Absolute symmetry isn't always necessary: A sleeve can be folded creating something that looks less clinical. Add details. When you are finished with your pencil underdrawing, you can then go over it with a fine line marker, outlining your drawing with a slightly heavier line marker. When finished, erase your pencil lines with a kneaded eraser.

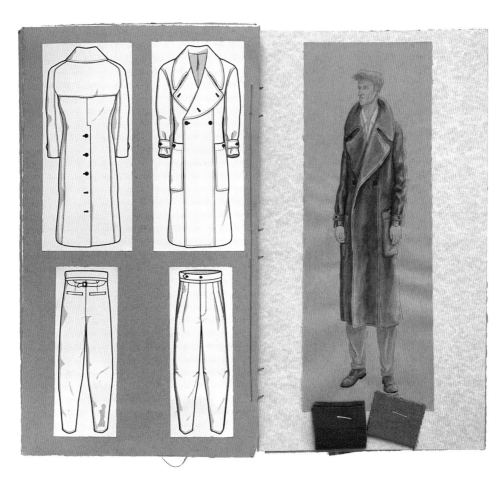

Figure 6.55 Artwork by Cody Cannon, 2019.

Figure 6.56a Hand-drawn flats by Renaldo Barnette.

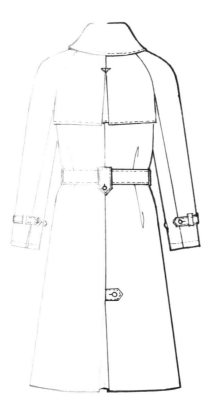

Figure 6.56b Hand-drawn flats by Renaldo Barnette.

Figure 6.56c Hand-drawn flats by Renaldo Barnette.

Figure 6.57a Hand-drawn flats by Renaldo Barnette.

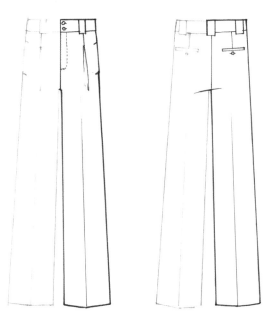

Figure 6.57b Hand-drawn flats by Renaldo Barnette.

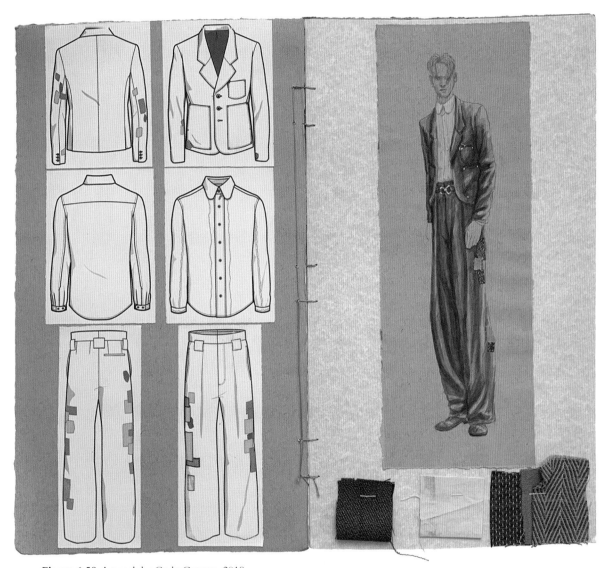

Figure 6.58 Artwork by Cody Cannon, 2019.

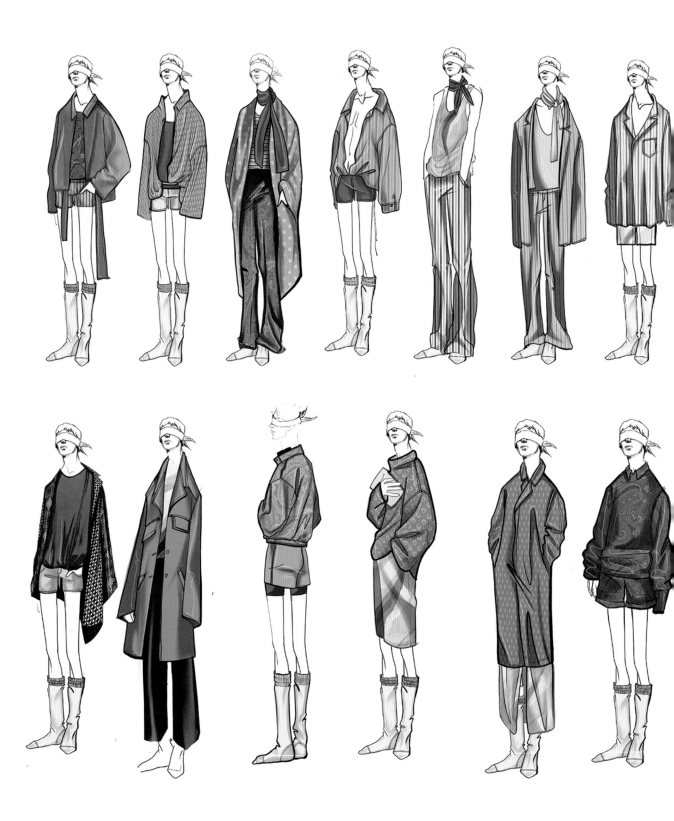

7

Digital Art

For many designers and illustrators, working across the digital platform has become as essential to their work today as the charcoal stub was to artists 100 years ago. The tools and functionality of the various apps and types of imaging software have introduced exciting new ways of drawing and painting. These digital media, when paired with the seemingly endless resources of the internet, can provide unlimited options for self-expression. Software such as Photoshop and Illustrator, used on the computer and paired with touch screens or tablets such as Wacom and other devices, as well as apps like Procreate, Tayasui Sketches, and more, allow for endless brush techniques. These can be used alongside pressure-sensitive touch screens or pencils such as Apple Pencil for a realistic, intuitive drawing experience.

Given that most of the world communicates digitally through texts and emails, smartphones and laptops, whether you use digital programs in your art or not, one can't deny the power and possibilities of this new reality. At the very least, a familiarity with digital media is absolutely essential for any designer or illustrator working today. Nevertheless, though the way we express ourselves visually may have changed, the basic skills of an artist or designer haven't. One must have a solid foundation of the principles of art and design as well as a good eye, solid draftsmanship, imagination, and skill. Whether you are finger painting on a cave wall or gliding a stylus across the glass surface of a tablet, you are still using the same lines, smudges, dots, and brushstrokes that humans have been using to describe the world around us for thousands of years. The look of the drawing utensil may be different, but the mark, and what it represents, is the same.

The basic concepts of figure drawing: Anatomy, line, shape, balance, and movement have been discussed and examined in earlier chapters. By understanding and incorporating these ideas into your digital drawings, you should be able to create compelling fashion art that communicates

Figure 7.1 Image courtesy of Rosario Catrimi. Toulemonde.

what you are trying to say. Many artists today combine both analog and digital techniques. The important thing is to be open to new ways of communicating visually, while also remaining coherent. Never forget that the clothed figure is your subject.

Since our primary focus is on the male fashion figure, it is best to focus on those programs and options that will help you achieve your goal. Like all art media, the more familiar you are with a particular software or app, the more likely you are to experiment. For artists who are just learning to draw, or even for an experienced artist of many years, there may sometimes be a steep learning curve when it comes to digital art. Learning and using any totally new media can be challenging. Experimentation leads to discovery, and discovery leads to skill building and confidence. By playing with brushes, layers,

Figure 7.2 Image courtesy of Brian Lane.

Figure 7.3 Image courtesy of Carlos Aponte.

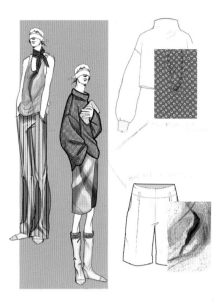

Figure 7.4 Image courtesy of Rosario Catrimi. Toulemonde.

tools, and options, you can expand your skill set while discovering what works for you and what doesn't.

Creating Digital Freehand Drawings

Just as a good fashion illustrator is an entire fashion editorial department in one person—a model coordinator, hair and make-up person, fashion editor, and art director—an iPad and an Apple Pencil can be as close to a complete art studio as one can get. Everything is at your fingertips in this "portable" studio: pencils, paints, erasers, endless surfaces, and effects. The main advantages of digital drawing over traditional art are the ease of redrawing and experimenting with non-destructive edits. With a stylus, or digital pencils like Apple Pencil, you can draw as if you were using a real pencil, with gradations of tone and density that mimic graphite or charcoal. Not only can you

mimic the effects of several media, but you can also amend or delete lines, or brushstrokes, with a quick press of the button, all without getting your hands or your workspace dirty.

DIGITAL DRAWING APPS

The **Procreate** digital illustration app is undoubtedly one of the most popular among professionals and students when combined with an iPad or similar tablets. With its suite of art tools and creative features, one can create work that looks convincingly as though it was created manually. One of the most powerful features of the app is the array of **Brushes**. There are a wide variety of brushes, and each brush has a different paint texture. There are pencil brushes, charcoal brushes, and watercolor paint brushes, just to name a few. All the brushes can easily be altered by opacity and size, and depending on how much pressure you apply, you can enlarge or diminish the width of a brushstroke, just as you would with a real brush. Tilt the brush one way for one effect and hold it for a different stroke. If, say, you are using a painting app like ArtRage, when you increase the pressure using the oil paint brush, the visible amount of the "paint" and the thickness and opaqueness of the paint being applied increases, looking exactly like an impasto brushstroke. As with most software and apps, Procreate allows you to customize your gesture controls and settings, so the experiences are personalized to your preferences.

Layers: We discussed layering as a technique in the previous chapter. To layer something is to gradually build a color with additional layers of light or dark color. This is true in almost every medium: watercolor, markers, or color pencils. It is also true in digital art. Digital layers are stacked on top of each other to separate parts of a

Figure 7.5 Image courtesy of Clifford Faust.

Figure 7.6 Armando Gabral in Raf Simons suit, 2008. Image courtesy of George Gozum.

painting or drawing from each other. It might be helpful to think of these layers as stacks of transparent paper. The layers overlap with each other, adding depth to an illustration. Depending on the density of the layers, the effect can be subtle or bold. One of the real advantages of working with digital layers is that, using clipping masks, opacity, adjustments, and blending modes, you can experiment endlessly with how the layers respond to one another, creating multitudes of possible combinations of effects.

Of course, the basic and most essential benefit of layers is that one can use a rough sketch or image as a guide for the layers above. When finished, you can delete the underdrawing layer. Backgrounds can be changed or kept without

changing the whole drawing. For digital collages, different surface textures, fabrics, and patterns can be scanned, saved, used, and edited independently, mimicking traditional collage techniques. For advanced editing, there is also the ability to save parts of a drawing that you like—say, a hand or a head—and then cut and paste those parts into a new document and finish the drawing there. In the past this was done to manual art with white-out paint, scissors, and paste. Now such corrections are immeasurably easier. Once finished, one could save the drawing by making a duplicate, and then experiment with other versions of the drawing. As with any medium, exploration and experimentation are a must, and you'll probably have fun doing it.

Figure 7.7 Image courtesy of Velicia Gourdin.

Figure 7.8 Image courtesy of Carlos Aponte.

Figure 7.9 Fingers Crossed, 2015. Image courtesy of George Gozum.

Other Drawing Apps

Sketchbook by Sketchbook Inc.: When this application is downloaded, it will give you a quick tutorial of where all the basic tools are. A favorite feature is the easy way it transfers your hand-drawn sketch to the screen. Once you've made a drawing, your camera doubles as a scanner, so you can import your art. The image imports with a transparent background so you can begin finishing the work in the app. **Art Set 4** is another well-liked basic drawing app. Because it feels like the physical tools you would use manually, this app is considered best for those new to digital illustration. It is free to download, but most of its tools are unlocked through Premium Pro features, which have an additional fee. The main attraction of this app is the ease with which the tools work together. It

has a good range of paper surfaces, and if you up-grade you'll have access to over 150 brushes, three-dimensional paint, fluid watercolor, a "wet" canvas tool, and dozens of other tools that you can customize. There are other drawing apps, of course: Tayasui Sketches Lite, ArtFlow, Adobe Illustrator Draw, SketchBook, Adobe Fresco, and Krita, to name a few. Again, your choice will depend on your skill set, your budget, and your student or professional needs.

Converting Hand-Drawn Figures into Digital Design Sketches

Many find it easier to draw a figure in pencil and then color it through Photoshop than to create the figure digitally from scratch. That's because

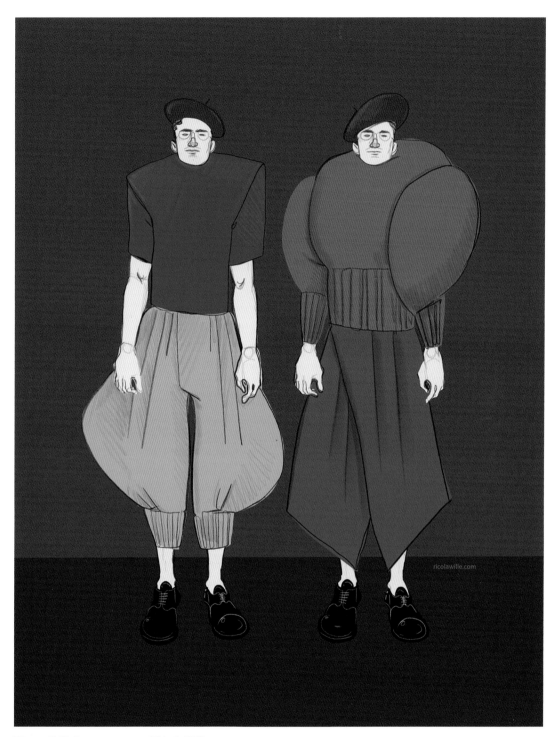

Figure 7.10 Image courtesy of Ricola Wille.

drawing the figure by hand and then rendering it digitally can feel both familiar and intuitive, like coloring a black-and-white figure in a children's coloring book. Scanning and retouching a hand-drawn illustration and then retouching or editing it is a relatively easy way of enhancing your artwork. One simple technique, if time is limited and you need a shortcut, starts by creating a pencil drawing. Once the drawing is finished, tape it to a lightbox or any light source. By taping a sheet of vellum or a thin sheet of watercolor paper on top of your drawing, you can then add your color wash, using the drawing underneath as a guide. Then scan both the drawing and the wash and merge them as separate layers in a Photoshop file. By setting the top layer to "Multiply," you can now refine your drawing by resizing, color correcting, or otherwise enhancing it by using any number of effects from the graphic software toolbox (the pen tool, brush tool, color enhancement, eraser, etc.).

Figure 7.11 Image courtesy of Rosario Catrimi. Toulemonde.

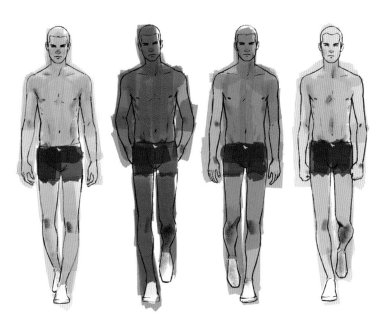

Figure 7.12 Image courtesy of Mitchell Van Au 2021.

Figure 7.13 Image courtesy of Mitchell Van Au 2021.

Figure 7.14 Image courtesy of Jusun Lee.

Another way to digitally render a hand-drawn figure is to use another Photoshop function, Waro, or Puppet Warp. While the basic warp function allows you to shape a part of your drawing using a basic grid, the Puppet Warp tool lets you twist and distort elements using more realistic precision. Scan a fabric or color wash, layer it onto your figure, and select edit; then choose either Warp or Puppet Warp. For Puppet Warp, you'll need to add "pins" for where you wish to create movement; then you can "drape the fabric" across the body as one might with an actual tailor's dummy, giving your illustration a more rendered, three-dimensional look. Once you are satisfied with the placement of the fabric, you can then add shadows and highlights for an even more three-dimensional effect.

Figure 7.15 Promostyl menswear illustration image courtesy of Mengjie Di. Mengjie Di—Promostyl.

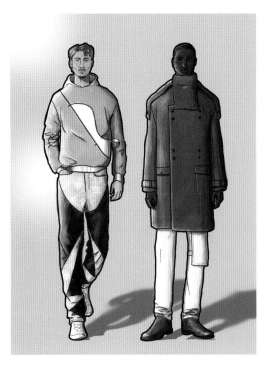

Figure 7.16 Image courtesy of Tyler Bubb, 2021.

Figure 7.17 Author, hand-drawn, and digital illustration using Puppet Warp.

Procreate also offers transformation tools and layers, so that the various elements of a figure and its hair, skin, and clothing can be rendered and edited in layers on top of the original line drawing. It's worth mentioning here, too, that while Illustrator is a vector program more commonly known for its technical features, it is also a strong tool for illustrators. Illustrator offers many powerful and intuitive brushes, effects, and layering features worth exploring to create illustrative and emotive artwork.

Developing Digital Garment Flats

Digital flats, like the hand-drawn flats discussed in the previous chapter, are also known as technical drawings or specs (short for technical specifications); these drawings allow manufacturers to produce a garment from the image alone. Vector-based graphics, like Adobe Illustrator, CorelDRAW, Manga Studio, and Photoshop, create geometric formations called "objects." Using points and line segments, myriad shapes and cures can be created and edited. These programs can create drawings with perfect symmetry, clean lines, and true-to-life proportions, while also quickly communicating information. Sophisticated digital drawing tools like these are essential in drawing digital flats. A successful flat is one in which a patternmaker, or sample machinist, would be able to assemble a garment from the image alone. Technical drawings are always made after the design has been produced.

Figure 7.18 Image courtesy of Bradley Erickson.

Figure 7.19 Flat illustrations by Bradley Erickson. Figures by author.

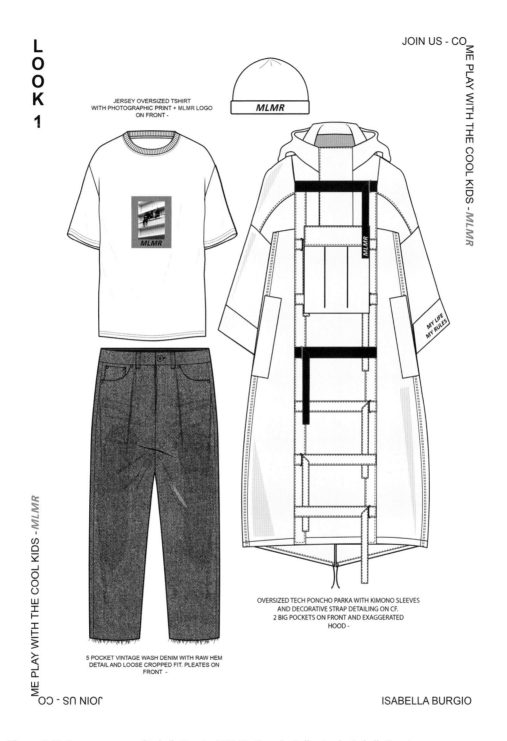

LOOK 1

JERSEY OVERSIZED TSHIRT
WITH PHOTOGRAPHIC PRINT + MLMR LOGO
ON FRONT -

MLMR

MLMR

MY LIFE
MY RULES

ME PLAY WITH THE COOL KIDS - *MLMR*

5 POCKET VINTAGE WASH DENIM WITH RAW HEM
DETAIL AND LOOSE CROPPED FIT. PLEATES ON
FRONT -

OVERSIZED TECH PONCHO PARKA WITH KIMONO SLEEVES
AND DECORATIVE STRAP DETAILING ON CF.
2 BIG POCKETS ON FRONT AND EXAGGERATED
HOOD -

ISABELLA BURGIO

Figure 7.20 Image courtesy of Isabella Burgio. MLMR Capsule Collection by Isabella Burgio.

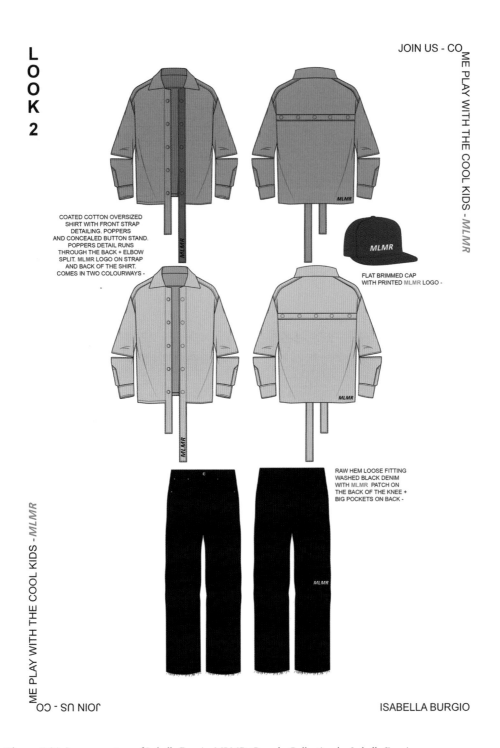

L
O
O
K
2

COATED COTTON OVERSIZED
SHIRT WITH FRONT STRAP
DETAILING. POPPERS
AND CONCEALED BUTTON STAND.
POPPERS DETAIL RUNS
THROUGH THE BACK + ELBOW
SPLIT. MLMR LOGO ON STRAP
AND BACK OF THE SHIRT.
COMES IN TWO COLOURWAYS -

FLAT BRIMMED CAP
WITH PRINTED MLMR LOGO -

RAW HEM LOOSE FITTING
WASHED BLACK DENIM
WITH MLMR PATCH ON
THE BACK OF THE KNEE +
BIG POCKETS ON BACK -

ISABELLA BURGIO

Figure 7.21 Image courtesy of Isabella Burgio. MLMR Capsule Collection by Isabella Burgio.

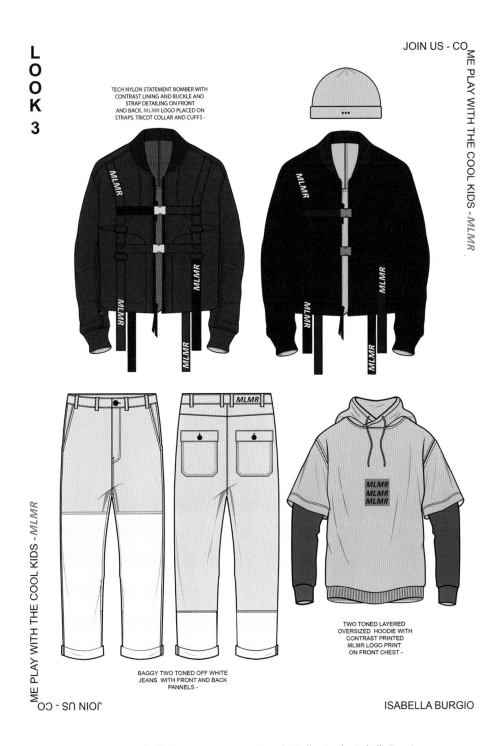

L
O
O
K
3

TECH NYLON STATEMENT BOMBER WITH
CONTRAST LINING AND BUCKLE AND
STRAP DETAILING ON FRONT
AND BACK. MLMR LOGO PLACED ON
STRAPS. TRICOT COLLAR AND CUFFS -

TWO TONED LAYERED
OVERSIZED HOODIE WITH
CONTRAST PRINTED
MLMR LOGO PRINT
ON FRONT CHEST -

BAGGY TWO TONED OFF WHITE
JEANS WITH FRONT AND BACK
PANNELS -

ME PLAY WITH THE COOL KIDS - *MLMR*
JOIN US - CO

ISABELLA BURGIO

Figure 7.22 Image courtesy of Isabella Burgio. MLMR Capsule Collection by Isabella Burgio.

Figure 7.23 Image courtesy of Emee Mathew.

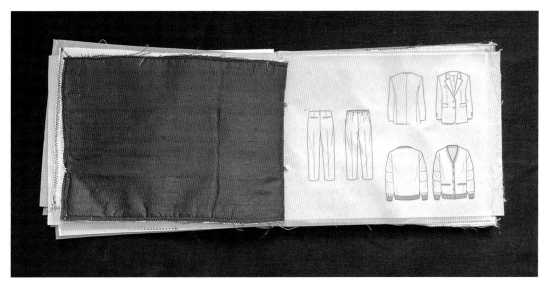

Figure 7.24 Image courtesy of Emee Mathew.

Figure 7.25 Image courtesy of Emee Mathew.

Figure 8.1 Francisco J. Cortés.

8

Profiles

CODY CANNON

How would you describe your current profession?

At the time of writing this, I am looking for work in Menswear Design or Concept Design. Unfortunately, I graduated from a fashion design program at a time when opportunities were few and far between due to the COVID-19 pandemic, making it very difficult to "break into" the industry.

What artistic training have you had?

Earlier in life, aside from the standard art classes in public school, I attended a small art school from grades seven to nine. There, I had several classes a week in drawing, painting, sculpture, etc. Many years later, I attended the Menswear Design program at the Fashion Institute of Technology in New York, where I took classes in life drawing and fashion illustration under inspired professors, one of whom was the author of this book.

What artists and/or menswear designers have inspired you?

Though unrelated to fashion design or illustration, I've always been enamored by European sculpture and engravings from the 16th to 18th centuries. There is a presence, a power, and a grace to these works, along with an exaggeration of musculature and anatomy, that I must imagine has guided my efforts in menswear illustration. Bernini, Michelangelo, and Hendrick Goltzius come to mind as the big names. Richard Powell is a modern illustrator that inspires me greatly; there is a fluidity and energy to his lines that I hope to one day come close to in my own work.

As for fashion design, I think the most personally influential names in my catalog of inspiration are menswear designers Christophe Lemaire, Issey Miyake, Woo Young Mi, and Giorgio Armani. Phoebe Philo's womenswear also deserves a place on that list; her work with Celine, particularly her silhouettes, was a revelation.

How would you describe your illustration style?

The first word to come to mind is "detailed." Prior to fashion design, I primarily drew with graphite and ink, aspiring toward the highly detailed European engravings I was so inspired by. This has bled into my fashion illustrations, though, as my style develops, I hope to "economize" detail and let my lines and brushstrokes flow to better communicate the drape I prioritize in my clothes.

What type of medium do you usually work in?

I sketch far more often than I complete fully rendered figures, and when sketching I use a mix of graphite, charcoal, chalk pastel, brush pens, and microns. For full illustrations, I prefer watercolor, with colored pencil where sharper detail is needed.

How important is drawing in your work?

I am a huge believer in exhaustively sketching out ideas in the development stages. The simple fact is: Experimenting with ideas (silhouettes, lapel and collar shapes, seam details, etc.) is a much faster process on a page than it is on fabric. By the time I cut anything, even for draping or for a mock-up, I want to have a direction in mind.

How important is the computer in your work?

The computer, and digital design generally, bookends my design work. I use it extensively in the research and development of the concept, then again in more technical design finalizations down the line. When working out the designs themselves, I prefer to work on paper or a dress form.

What, in your opinion, makes a good fashion drawing?

Clear communication of the attitude, energy, and style of the design. The pose should suggest the attitude of the collection, and if a look or piece is defined by its texture or drape, that should be evident in the medium, line, and stroke in the illustration.

What is your advice for any beginner menswear illustrator or designer?

Draw constantly, always carry a sketchbook around with you, and don't be afraid to try new mediums.

CARLOS APONTE

@carlosvisualdiary, @_tape_recorder, illustrationdivision.com

How would you describe your current profession?

I would describe myself as a creative or an artist. As much as those words have been used and abused, they cover more ground for me. Definitions in the illustration world, art, or even gender have been blurred or changed. I can't even describe what I do because of the variety of the projects I've been hired to do. In one year, I can do a children's book, windows for a store, a logo for a company, fashion art, or a storyboard for animation.

What artistic training have you had?

I trained as a fashion illustrator, but I've worn many hats throughout my life. I was painting in high school; then I did fashion design, political cartoons, comic strips, graphic design, learning a bit of animation and filmmaking, and, of course, fashion illustration. I believe, and I have the experience to prove it, that one discipline informs the other. There is a friend of mine that always tells me that whatever I do is always fashionable. All of that is tied to my training in fashion. Recently I was hired to work on a window for Bergdorf, the New York store, and thanks to my understanding of patternmaking, I could solve some design elements that had nothing to do with a dress.

What artists and/or menswear designers have inspired you?

I've been fortunate to have met Antonio, who supplied me with the desire and inspiration for my career. Like me, he was from Puerto Rico, and that added to my resolution in succeeding. Later, Jack Potter and Anna Ishikawa were two brilliant artists and professors at FIT and the School of Visual Arts. Jack's classes stretched my views to different areas; he made me see things from different angles and be fearless in my work. He broke the illusion of reality. Without this idea, I could have never done my masking-tape fashion art. He revolutionized my brain!

How would you describe your illustration style?

My style? I could describe it as bold, graphic, shape oriented.

What type of medium do you usually work in?

I could use Tombow brush markers one day, Posca markers the next, masking tape, ink, brush, or digital. I like to try new things.

How important is drawing in your work?

I've drawn since I was a kid, and I still do. I need to practice that basic foundation almost every day to stay sharp.

How important is the computer in your work?

I use digital for experimenting and my children's book; it makes things easy. I don't particularly appreciate that I rely a bit too much on it. I like to have originals and retain my line confidence.

What, in your opinion, makes a good fashion drawing?

A fashion drawing for a fashion designer is about making the idea of a dress alive. A fashion illustration is about capturing the essence of a dress and telling a story.

What is your advice for any beginner menswear illustrator or designer?

Draw constantly, learn from the masters of the past. Fall in love with the language of drawing and its many elements. Make this a meaningful relationship in your life if you are really serious about this.

MENGJIE DI

How would you describe your current profession?

I am a professor in the Fashion Department at Savannah College of Art and Design. I have held this position since 2012. Aside from teaching, I freelance for fashion companies globally and create personal artwork.

What artistic training have you had?

I received most of my artistic training from the fine art school I attended during the first year of college in China. Other skills have been a result of self-teaching and discovering.

What artists and/or menswear designers have inspired you?

There are lots of artists who have inspired me through different stages of my creative career. Wassily Kandinsky was the most influential artist during my first year of college. I did several big studies on his works, including *Composition 8*, *Hard in Soft*, *Original Color Collotype*, etc. This was my earliest artistic discovery, and I was obsessed with all his works and art theories. As my creative searching has evolved, I have discovered many artists who influenced my understanding about art, such as Marlene Dumas, Willem De Kooning, Gerhard Richter, Michaël Borremans, Georgia O'Keeffe, and more. In recent years, I focus more on Asian artists especially Chinese and Japanese, for example Lang Shining (Giuseppe Castiglione),

Hokusai, Mao Yan, Yu Hong, etc. The list just goes on and on.

As far as menswear designers go, I enjoy Damir Doma, Walter Van Beirendonck, Bode, Juun.J, Raf Simon in collaboration with Sterling Ruby, and many more.

How would you describe your illustration style?

I have two different illustration styles. When I freelance for fashion companies, I usually keep the styles commercial and straightforward. My personal works are quite experimental and expressive.

What type of medium do you usually work in?

I work with multiple mediums, including digital, watercolor, acrylic, oil pastel, graphite, etc.

How important is drawing in your work?

Drawing provides me with an avenue for personal expression. It also has a calming effect, in that I can dive into my drawing and get away from the everyday stresses of life. In the classroom, I enjoy drawing demonstrations, where I explain techniques and skills to eager learners.

How important is the computer in your work?

A computer is a tool just like pencil and brushes. It allows efficient work processes, multiple revisions, and quick changes. It has become the main tool for lots of my works.

What, in your opinion, makes a good fashion drawing?

In my opinion, a proper representation of a good fashion drawing can demonstrate powerful emotions and mastery of mediums. A good drawing can leave viewers with a mesmerizing visual experience.

What is your advice for any beginner menswear illustrator or designer?

My advice for a beginner menswear illustrator is very simple: persistence and determination. To reference a historical quote: "Nothing in this world can take the place of persistence. Talent will not; There is nothing more common than talented but unsuccessful men. Wisdom without reward is almost as conventional as a proverb. Education will not; the world is full of educated bums. Persistence and determination are omnipotent." —Calvin Coolidge.

BRIAN LANE

@blanedesign

How would you describe your current profession?

Currently, I am the Men's Outerwear Designer for the retailer Brooks Brothers and the Senior Designer of Men's and Women's Uniforms for United Airlines, along with other uniform projects, and I have been the house illustrator for cross-collateral projects for Brooks Brothers for the past eleven-plus years.

What artistic training have you had?

I've attended the High School of Art and Design for General Illustration and Design, and Fashion Institute of Technology (FIT) for Fashion Illustration.

What artists and/or menswear designers have inspired you?

On the illustration side, it would be Bob Peak, Frank Frazetta, Jim Steranko.

On the fashion side, Antonio Lopez, George Stavrinos, *Lamont O'Neal.

For designers, Armani, Ralph Lauren, Kim Jones, Virgil Abloh, and the list goes on.

How would describe your illustration style?

Sometimes it depends on the assignment... I've been loose and sometimes very tight. But I would say a bit "Retro," with a looser hand over time.

What type of mediums do you usually work in?

Pen and ink, watercolor and marker, color pencil, and Adobe Illustrator.

How important is drawing in your work?

VERY! In my role I must illustrate ideas in a way that is readily understood by the widest audience possible. I work on collateral illustrations for company advertisements, so the art that I do will be seen worldwide.

How important is the computer in your work?

Very! In the systems here everything is inter-connected and easily shared: it's the only way to work these days. It's a step process that goes from concept to finished product.

What, in your opinion, makes a good fashion drawing?

As in any type of art, it must be inspiring and should draw you in ... And then you see the clothing—which always should be "Legible" ... If you can do that along with exhibiting your personal "Style," you've got a winner.

What is the advice for any beginner menswear illustrator or designer?

To study other illustrators and designers. Whether you like them or not. They are at the top for a reason. Try to understand why. Pay attention to things around you like clothing and how it is worn, or social media. You can always learn something new every day, if you're open to it. But keep your individual style and be open to pivoting here and there. That's what brings out the artist's or designer's creativity.

RYAN MCMENAMY

ryanmcmenamy.com

How would you describe your current profession?

I would describe my profession as being both an artist and an illustrator.

What artistic training have you had?

I went to Parsons School of Design, majoring in illustration.

What artists and/or menswear designers have inspired you?

I've always been inspired by the art of early 1900s Paris, especially Toulouse-Lautrec. The drawing of everyday street culture combined fashion, illustration, and fine art all at once.

How would you describe your illustration style?

I would describe my work as being traditional life-drawing-based but extremely edited and reduced, leaving a graphic result.

What type of medium do you usually work in?

When drawing I work in charcoal, and when painting I work in gouache.

How important is drawing in your work?

My work almost only consists of drawing, so it is essential to me.

How important is the computer in your work?

My computer is of almost no use in my work.

What, in your opinion, makes a good fashion drawing?

What makes a good fashion drawing to me is the same as what makes any nice drawing in general. Line quality, composition, rendering, gesture, attitude, etc.

What is your advice for any beginner menswear illustrator or designer?

My advice would be to keep at it, and keep drawing.

EMEE MATHEW

emeemathew.com

How would you describe your current profession?

I used to work as an assistant designer until last month. I have moved to Vancouver, Canada, to pursue a Post-Baccalaureate in Technical Apparel Design.

What artistic training have you had?

I didn't really receive formal training until I started college. But I was very interested as a teenager. So, I started learning by watching tutorials on YouTube, reading books, and sketching people on the streets every day for at least 30 minutes.

What artists and/or menswear designers have inspired you?

One of the first illustration books that I ever read was by Anna Kiper. She was an inspiration to me, and in fact I chose to go to Fashion Institute of Technology because she taught there. Another illustrator and designer who inspired me was Sal Cesarani, whose classes I had the privilege to attend as a menswear student. Designers like Dries Van Noten and brands like Brunello Cucinelli continue to inspire me.

How would you describe your illustration style?

I taught myself how to draw by observing and later from my professors at school who had a more traditional formal training. It has always been a mix between the traditional eight-head and my tendency to revert to sketching head-waist-knee proportions.

What type of medium do you usually work in?

I usually work with markers. Specifically, Prismacolors. Those were the first markers I ever bought, and I still use them.

How important is drawing in your work?

A picture is worth a thousand words. Drawing helps me translate my ideas and has always been a great way to communicate with others. Be it fit notes, pattern specifications, or even fabric sourcing, I always make quick sketches.

How important is the computer in your work?

With the transition to offsite learning and working, I switched and starting practicing more with sketching solely on Photoshop.

Investing in a better tablet helped, and I spent more time learning how to redraw on a different platform.

Initially, it used to be vital only to the extent of certain pattern fills and sketch adjustments.

What, in your opinion, makes a good fashion drawing?

I have always been a stickler for proportions. Even in school, when the professors asked me to explore proportion play, I always returned to the traditional proportions I was most comfortable with.

What is your advice for any beginner menswear illustrator or designer?

Practice, practice, practice. It is one of the most common words of advice out there, but it is also the most vital thing out there. I still spend every weekend sitting in a cafe or park observing people and sketching them mid-motion. And the more I draw, the more I learn from mistakes and improve myself.

Also, never be afraid to explore different mediums, because at the end of the day, if your ideas are translated and understood, it is a job well done.

FRANCISCO CORTÉS

@franciscoj.cortes, facebook. com/franciscojavier. cortesiglesias

How would you describe your current profession?

Currently, I work as a fashion design teacher at the San Telmo School of Art and Design (Malaga, Spain). I teach Fashion Design Projects and Costume Projects for the Scene.

The teaching profession for me is exciting, a vocation (that I did not know I had until I began to exercise it). It is a job that I am passionate about. Being in contact with my students rejuvenates my ideas, keeps me awake and curious about the world ... and feeling part of their training, contributing my experiences and my knowledge, excites me.

Drawing has always been part of my life, although professionally I have not dedicated myself to it. Illustration has come to me a bit late, and it has been through social networks that I have started to spread my work. And it's another passion for me!

What artistic training have you had?

In matters of drawing and fashion design, as well as in my side as an illustrator, I consider myself almost self-taught. I have not had specific artistic training. I have been drawing since I can remember, and fashion design has always been a passion—one first discovered when I was twelve or thirteen years old. In my college years, I trained as an art historian, and years later I trained as a fashion design technician, where I perfected my drawing and my training as a designer, working as a designer assistant at a fashion brand for seven years.

What artists and/or menswear designers have inspired you?

Menswear design began to interest me a bit later than womenswear design. My interest has always been in French haute couture and its big names like Yves Saint Laurent (my favorite designer),

Balenciaga, Dior, Givenchy, Ungaro, Chanel, and many others.

In men's fashion I have always liked the work of more alternative designers (although my style is more classic), such as the Japanese (Yohji Yamamoto, Issey Miyake, Comme des Garçons) but also the sartorial style of Ozwald Boateng or Francesco Smalto, the avant-garde by Rick Owens or Thom Browne, the contemporaneity of JW Anderson, Kim Jones, the late Virgil Abloh, the genderless style and freedom of Jean-Paul Gaultier, the theatrical and ironic style of Moschino (with Franco Moschino first, Rossella Jardini later, and now Jeremy Scott), the provocation of Alexander McQueen or the eroticism of Tom Ford and DSquared[2]. Many references ... it seems like a review of Fashion History (laughs). Now I also pay a lot of attention to young designers like Ludovic de Saint Sernin or Andrea Grossi.

How would you describe your illustration style?

I think my illustration style is a "classic" style, based on a precise drawing supported by the stroke, anatomically correct and quite descriptive. Especially for male illustration. When I draw or illustrate women's fashion, I allow myself some stylistic licenses, with a somewhat more fluid and free drawing. I don't know ... it's a bit difficult for me to speak and judge my own style of illustration. I think that for me, the line is more important than the color: the gesture defined by the line, the definition of black on white, the graphism ... I pay attention a lot to Gruau, Eric, David Downton, Michael Vollbracht, Robert Passantino, George Stavrinos, or Marc-Antoine Coulon, among many other illustrators who have influenced me.

What type of medium do you usually work in?

In technical terms, I work mostly with pencil, pen, marker, and watercolor markers ... on paper and in all formats. I draw on any supports, surfaces, and sizes (laughs). Above all, I love to draw ... although lately I have little time to do it!

How important is drawing in your work?

It's fundamental! It is the first form of approaching, of expression of the idea ... Some colleagues think that for fashion design, knowing how to draw is not the most important thing. They take the fabric and place it directly on a bust and begin to model. That's okay. But for me everything begins with drawing, with the expression on paper of the idea, of the inspiration ... As I'm a teacher of Fashion Design Projects and Costume Projects for the Scene, for me, drawing is everything: it communicates the idea, the appearance of the design, the silhouette, the volume, the quality of the fabric, the "allure" of the design, the appearance of the stage character ...

Drawing is the way to communicate what fashion means to me: culture, art, design, a certain sense of taste, the beauty, the aesthetics representing the spirit of our time, the "zeitgeist" ... I love how fashion illustration is once again recovering the important role it had in the communication and broadcasting of fashion in its golden years of the 20th century.

How important is the computer in your work?

For my work as an illustrator, I don't use the computer. I am a prehistoric illustrator (laughs). I like digital illustration work and the possibilities that computer design programs offer for fashion illustration. But it's not my way. I love the freedom that manual tracing offers me, the nuances I get, the lack of control over the final result… also, I don't always carry my computer with me! But, a notebook and a pencil, yes (laughs).

What, in your opinion, makes a good fashion drawing?

It is difficult to pin down! For me, it is important that it be descriptive and clear in the representation of the formal aspects of the design, the silhouette and the volumes… if what we are talking about is fashion design. A correct proportion, a well-represented anatomy, etc.: these are less important to me.

However, if we talk about fashion illustration, I think it is important that it captures the "allure" of design, evokes sensations, and tells us something beyond how the shape or structure of the design is… the emotional part!

What is your advice for any beginner menswear illustrator or designer?

I don't really like giving advice! In my classes as a teacher, in my work as an illustrator, I think the key is passion: doing what you like, not being afraid of making mistakes or doing things differently from how others do. Be true to yourself and work, be constant, have something (or a lot) of talent and … work, work, and work. Training is also important, no matter how you do it. But, above all, passion for what you do and doing the best you can. At the end, yes, I have given advice! (laughs)

BIBLIOGRAPHY

Bargiel, Rejane, Nissen, Sylvie. *Gruau: Portraits of Men*. Assouline Publishing, New York. 2012

Blackman, Cally. *100 Years of Fashion Illustration*. Laurence King Publishing, London. 2015

Borrelli, Laird. *Stylishly Drawn: Contemporary Fashion Illustration*. Harry N. Abrams, New York. 2000

Boston, Lloyd. *Men of Color: Fashion, History, Fundamentals*. Artisan, New York. 1998

Breward, Christopher. *The Suit: Form, Function and Style*. Reaktion Books Ltd, London. 2016

Brommer, Gerald. *Collage Techniques: A Guide for Artists and Illustrators*. Watson–Guptill Publications, New York. 1994

Caranicas, Paul. *Antonio's People*. Thames & Hudson Ltd, London. 2004

Ceccarelli, Giuseppe. *Menswear: 20 Timeless Elements of Style*. White Star Publishers, Vercelli. 2016

Chenoune, Farid. *A History of Men's Fashion*. Flammarion, Paris. 1993

Contini, Mila. *Fashion: From Ancient Egypt to the Present Day*. The Odyssey Press, New York. 1965

Dawber, Martin. *Imagemakers: Cutting Edge Fashion Illustration*. Mitchell Beazley, London. 2004

Downton, David. *Masters of Fashion Illustration*. Laurence King Publishing, London. 2010

Ford, Richard Thompson. *Dress Codes: How the Laws of Fashion Made History*. Simon & Schuster Paperbacks, New York. 2021

Foster, Walter T. *Fashion Illustrations 1920–1950*. Dover Publications, Inc., New York. 2010

Greenburg, O'Malley Zack. *Three Kings: Diddy, Dr. Dre, Jay-Z and Hip-Hop's Multibillion Dollar Rise*. Little, Brown and Company, New York. 2018

Harrison, Hazel. *The Encyclopedia of Watercolor Techniques*. Search Press, Tunbridge Wells, UK. 2018

Jardine, Alison. *Make Great Art on Your iPad: Draw, Paint and Share*. Ilex Press, London. 2017

Kilroy, Richard. *Menswear Illustration*. Thames & Hudson Ltd, London. 2015

Lipmann, Anthony. *Divinely Elegant: The World of Ernst Dryden*. Pavilion Books Ltd, London. 1989

Mackrell, Alice. *An Illustrated History of Fashion*. Quite Specific Media Group Ltd, New York. 1997

Massen, Michael. *The Artist's Guide to Drawing the Clothed Figure*. Watson–Guptill Publications, New York. 2011

Moers, Ellen. *The Dandy: Brummell to Beerbohm*. University of Nebraska Press, Lincoln, NE. 1978

Packer, William. *Fashion Drawing in Vogue*. Coward–McCann, Inc., New York. 1983

Ramos, Juan. *Antonio: 60, 70, 80: Three Decades in Style*. Schirmer Art Books, Munich. 1995

Raynes, John. *Figure Drawing*. Bonanza Books, New York. 1981

Reed, Walt. *The Figure*. Weathervane Books, New York. 1989

Reinert, Rachel. *Color Workshop*. Mixed Media Resources, New York. 2017

Robinson, Julian. *The Golden Age of Style: Art Deco Fashion Illustration*. Orbis Publishing Ltd, London. 1976

Schau, Michael. *J.C. Leyendecker*. Watson-Guptill Publications, New York. 1974

Sloane, Eunice. *Illustrating Fashion*. Harper & Row Publishers, New York. 1977

Spitz, Bob. *The Beatles*. Little, Brown and Company, New York. 2018

Steinhart, Peter. *The Undressed Art: Why We Draw*. Vintage Books, London. 2004

Tallon, Kevin. *Digital Fashion Illustration*. Batsford, London. 2008

Yajima, Isao. *Mode Drawing: Costume*, 2nd ed. Books Nippan, Carson, CA. 1988

Ziegler, Philip. *King Edward VIII*. Alfred A. Knopf, New York. 1991

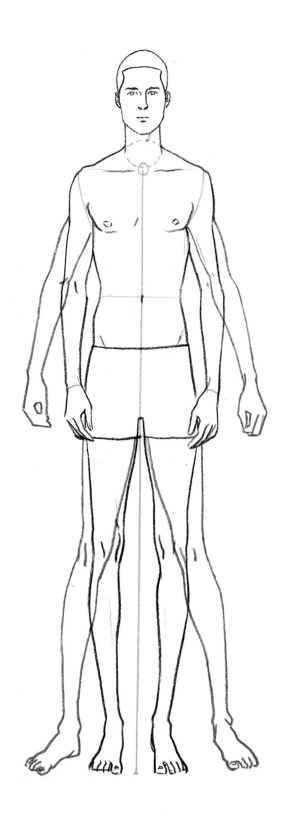

ABOUT THE AUTHOR

Lamont O'Neal was born in Brooklyn, New York. He began drawing as a child, inspired by comic books and fashion magazines. After attending the High School of Art & Design, he won a scholarship to Parsons School of Design to study fashion design and fashion illustration, both of which continue to influence his style. In his thirty-year-plus career, O'Neal has been published in nearly every aspect of the fashion world, including the magazines *Cosmopolitan*, *New York*, *GQ*, *Playboy*, and *Essence*. He has worked with the likes of Oscar de la Renta, David Chu, American Eagle, and Polo Ralph Lauren, and has frequently contributed covers for Vogue Butterick. His credits also include portraiture, children's books, and illustrations for Revlon, Random House, Estée Lauder, William Morrow Publishing, Nordstrom, Simon and Schuster, J. Walter Thompson, Lord & Taylor, Maybelline, and Vogue Knitting.

O'Neal's work has been recognized by the Society of Illustrators in New York. He lives and draws in Yardley, Pennsylvania.

MENSWEAR GLOSSARY

Bespoke The process of creating a garment entirely from scratch without using any pre-existing patterns.

Blazer A jacket that is in between a suit jacket and a sport jacket in terms of fit and formality. Less formal than a suit jacket, but not as informal as a sport jacket. Traditionally, blazers were navy, but can be tan, gray, or even plaid. They usually have metal buttons.

Break The fold in the fabric at the bottom of the pant leg where it hits the shoe.

Full break The traditional pant length that creates a single full fold inward and results in the fabric covering over half the back of the shoe.

Half break A pant length that only creates a slight fold inward, so the bottom of the trouser leg covers only the top quarter of the back of the shoe.

Button-down collars Collar points that are fastened by buttons on the front of the shirt. Introduced by Brooks Brothers in 1896.

Button stance Where the top button of a jacket rests. Typically, this would sit between one and three fingers above the belly button.

Canvas A layer of fabric in between the outer fabric and the lining of the jacket's front panels, usually made of wool and horsehair. This helps support the shape of the jacket and is loosely stitched to the fabric to allow for free movement.

Full canvas The canvas is sewn into the front panel for the most structure.

Fused A fused suit's inner structural layer is glued to the fabric rather than being sewn in.

Half canvas The canvas is sewn only into the chest area of the jacket, making it more lightweight than a full canvas jacket.

Collar gap A gap that exists between the collar of a jacket and the wearer's neck. This means that the jacket doesn't fit properly.

Collar roll A roll of fabric on the jacket at the back of the neck. This is an indication that the jacket doesn't fit properly.

Custom An item of clothing that is made to measure rather than being purchased off the rack. This includes made-to-measure and bespoke.

Double-breasted A jacket with two columns of buttons. The fabric overlays when closed. It may have four or six buttons. A double-breasted suit almost always has a peak lapel.

Drape How a suit hangs on the body.

Flap pocket Pockets built into the jacket with a flap covering the opening.

Flat-front Trousers without pleats.

French cuffs Twice as long as regular cuffs, French cuffs fold back and fasten with cufflinks or fabric knots.

Gorge A seam that joins the collar to a lapel.

Gusset A triangular piece of fabric inserted at a seam to add strength and durability to a garment

Inseam The measurement from the inside of the pants at the crotch to the bottom of the pant leg.

Lapel The folded fabric on the front of a jacket that is attached to the collar.

Notch lapel Sometimes called a step lapel, it is sewn onto the collar at an angle creating a "notch" or V-shape.

Peak lapel A lapel that is sewn into the collar so that it points upwards, usually extending beyond the collar.

Shawl lapel A continuous collar without any separation between the collar and the lapel.

Made-to-measure An item of clothing that has been made to the precise measurements and requirements of the wearer.

Nap The raised surface found projecting from a fabric. Typically produced by intentionally brushing or occurring naturally during weaving.

Outseam The measurement from the top of the waistband on the outside edge of the pants to the bottom of the leg.

Patch pocket Jacket pockets that are sewn onto the outer fabric of the suit using the same suit fabric.

Pitch stitch Subtle hand stitching around the lapel, pockets, and cuffs of a suit or jacket.

Pleat A small section of folded fabric on the front of the trousers along the waist. Pants may have a single or double pleat.

Ready to wear – Also known as "off the rack," this term refers to garments that have not been custom made and exist as part of the regular stock in the store.

Rise The difference between the outseam and the inseam measurement.

Roped shoulder Sometimes known as the structured shoulder on a suit jacket, roped shoulders have a sleeve head that extends beyond the shoulder, creating a lip.

Single-breasted A jacket with a single column of buttons. It may have one, two, or three buttons.

Soft shoulder Also known as an unstructured shoulder, these use very little or no padding and have no roping.

Sport jacket Also known as a sport coat, or sports jacket. Sport jackets are less formal than blazers or suit jackets.

Spread collar A variation on a standard men's shirt collar, with a wide spread between the points.

Suit jacket Suit jackets are always part of a full suit, either two-piece or three-piece, and tend to be longer and more structured than a blazer or a sport jacket.

Tailored clothing Refers to any item of clothing that is made to fit the shape of a person's body. In menswear this would typically include suits, sport jackets, trousers, vests and occasionally outerwear.

Three-piece suit A suit that includes jacket, vest, and trousers.

Ticket pocket A small pocket located just above the right pocket on a jacket.

Two-piece suit A suit that includes only jacket and trousers.

Tuxedo A formal suit that may be two or three pieces. The jacket typically has a silk or satin collar and lapel, and the trousers have a silk stripe down the side. Also known as a dinner jacket.

Unfinished hem Pants with a raw edge at the bottom that must be hemmed.

Vents Vertical slits on the back of a jacket that allow it to drape naturally and comfortably when sitting and moving.

    Double vent Also known as side vents. Vents on either side of the back panel of the jacket.

    Single vent Also known as a center vent. A vent down the middle of the back panel of the jacket.

Warp Warp is the vertical threading of a garment. In contrast, **weft** is the horizontal threading.

Welt pocket Also known as a besom pocket, a welt pocket is a bound flat pocket that has a finish with a welt or reinforced border along the edge of the fabric. Often found in the front of a man's jacket, with a handkerchief tucked in.

Yoke The section along the shoulders at the shirt that connects all the other parts of the shirt.

INDEX

Note: Page locators in *italic* refer to figure captions.